Lewis and Clark
and the Route to the Pacific

General Editor

William H. Goetzmann
Jack S. Blanton, Sr., Chair in History
  University of Texas at Austin

Consulting Editor

Tom D. Crouch
Chairman, Department of Aeronautics
  National Air and Space Museum
  Smithsonian Institution

WORLD EXPLORERS

Lewis and Clark
and the Route to the Pacific

Seamus Cavan

Introductory Essay by Michael Collins

CHELSEA HOUSE PUBLISHERS

New York · Philadelphia

On the cover   Map of the territory covered by the Lewis and Clark expedition; portraits of Meriwether Lewis (left) and William Clark.

Chelsea House Publishers
Editor-in-Chief   Remmel Nunn
Managing Editor   Karyn Gullen Browne
Copy Chief   Juliann Barbato
Picture Editor   Adrian G. Allen
Art Director   Maria Epes
Deputy Copy Chief   Mark Rifkin
Assistant Art Director   Noreen Romano
Series Design   Loraine Machlin
Manufacturing Manager   Gerald Levine
Systems Manager   Lindsey Ottman
Production Manager   Joseph Romano
Production Coordinator   Marie Claire Cebrián

World Explorers
Senior Editor   Sean Dolan

***Staff for* LEWIS AND CLARK AND THE ROUTE TO THE PACIFIC**
Copy Editor   Joseph Roman
Editorial Assistant   Martin Mooney
Picture Researcher   Lisa Kirchner
Senior Designer   Basia Niemczyc

7   9   8   6

Library of Congress Cataloging-in-Publication Data

Cavan, Seamus
   Lewis and Clark and the route to the Pacific/Cavan, Seamus
      p.   cm.—(World explorers)
   Includes bibliographical references and index.
   Summary: An account of the 1804–6 Lewis and Clark expedition that explored the unknown Louisiana Purchase territory and the Pacific Northwest from St. Louis to the mouth of the Columbia River.
   ISBN 0-7910-1327-8
         0-7910-1538-6 (pbk.)
   1. Lewis and Clark Expedition (1804–6)—Juvenile literature.
2. Lewis, Meriwether, 1774–1809—Juvenile literature.   3. Clark, William, 1770–1838—Juvenile literature.   [1. Lewis and Clark Expedition (1804–6)   2. Lewis, Meriwether, 1774–1809.
3. Clark, William, 1770–1838.]   I. Title.   II. Series.
F592.7.M73   1991   90-23479
917.804′2—dc20   CIP
                                                    AC

CONTENTS

WORLD EXPLORERS

THE EARLY EXPLORERS

Herodotus and the Explorers of the Classical Age
Marco Polo and the Medieval Explorers
The Viking Explorers

THE FIRST GREAT AGE OF DISCOVERY

Jacques Cartier, Samuel de Champlain, and the Explorers of Canada
Christopher Columbus and the First Voyages to the New World
From Coronado to Escalante: The Explorers of the Spanish Southwest
Hernando de Soto and the Explorers of the American South
Sir Francis Drake and the Struggle for an Ocean Empire
Vasco da Gama and the Portuguese Explorers
La Salle and the Explorers of the Mississippi
Ferdinand Magellan and the Discovery of the World Ocean
Pizarro, Orellana, and the Exploration of the Amazon
The Search for the Northwest Passage
Giovanni da Verrazano and the Explorers of the Atlantic Coast

THE SECOND GREAT AGE OF DISCOVERY

Roald Amundsen and the Quest for the South Pole
Daniel Boone and the Opening of the Ohio Country
Captain James Cook and the Explorers of the Pacific
The Explorers of Alaska
John Charles Frémont and the Great Western Reconnaissance
Alexander von Humboldt, Colossus of Exploration
Lewis and Clark and the Route to the Pacific
Alexander Mackenzie and the Explorers of Canada
Robert Peary and the Quest for the North Pole
Zebulon Pike and the Explorers of the American Southwest
John Wesley Powell and the Great Surveys of the American West
Jedediah Smith and the Mountain Men of the American West
Henry Stanley and the European Explorers of Africa
Lt. Charles Wilkes and the Great U.S. Exploring Expedition

THE THIRD GREAT AGE OF DISCOVERY

Apollo to the Moon
The Explorers of the Undersea World
The First Men in Space
The Mission to Mars and Beyond
Probing Deep Space

CHELSEA HOUSE PUBLISHERS

Into the Unknown

Michael Collins

It is difficult to define most eras in history with any precision, but not so the space age. On October 4, 1957, it burst on us with little warning when the Soviet Union launched *Sputnik*, a 184-pound cannonball that circled the globe once every 96 minutes. Less than 4 years later, the Soviets followed this first primitive satellite with the flight of Yury Gagarin, a 27-year-old fighter pilot who became the first human to orbit the earth. The Soviet Union's success prompted President John F. Kennedy to decide that the United States should "land a man on the moon and return him safely to earth" before the end of the 1960s. We now had not only a space age but a space race.

I was born in 1930, exactly the right time to allow me to participate in Project Apollo, as the U.S. lunar program came to be known. As a young man growing up, I often found myself too young to do the things I wanted—or suddenly too old, as if someone had turned a switch at midnight. But for Apollo, 1930 was the perfect year to be born, and I was very lucky. In 1966 I enjoyed circling the earth for three days, and in 1969 I flew to the moon and laughed at the sight of the tiny earth, which I could cover with my thumbnail.

How the early explorers would have loved the view from space! With one glance Christopher Columbus could have plotted his course and reassured his crew that the world was indeed round. In 90 minutes Magellan could have looked down at every port of call in the *Victoria's* three-year circumnavigation of the globe. Given a chance to map their route from orbit, Lewis and Clark could have told President Jefferson that there was no easy Northwest Passage but that a continent of exquisite diversity awaited their scrutiny.

In a physical sense, we have already gone to most places that we can. That is not to say that there are not new adventures awaiting us deep in the sea or on the red plains of Mars, but more important than reaching new places will be understanding those we have already visited. There are vital gaps in our understanding of how our planet works as an ecosystem and how our planet fits into the infinite order of the universe. The next great age may well be the age of assimilation, in which we use microscope and telescope to evaluate what we have discovered and put that knowledge to use. The adventure of being first to reach may be replaced by the satisfaction of being first to grasp. Surely that is a form of exploration as vital to our well-being, and perhaps even survival, as the distinction of being the first to explore a specific geographical area.

The explorers whose stories are told in the books of this series did not just sail perilous seas, scale rugged mountains, traverse blistering deserts, dive to the depths of the ocean, or land on the moon. Their voyages and expeditions were journeys of mind as much as of time and distance, through which they—and all of mankind—were able to reach a greater understanding of our universe. That challenge remains, for all of us. The imperative is to see, to understand, to develop knowledge that others can use, to help nurture this planet that sustains us all. Perhaps being born in 1975 will be as lucky for a new generation of explorer as being born in 1930 was for Neil Armstrong, Buzz Aldrin, and Mike Collins.

The Reader's Journey

William H. Goetzmann

This volume is one of a series that takes us with the great explorers of the ages on bold journeys over the oceans and the continents and into outer space. As we travel along with these imaginative and courageous journeyers, we share their adventures and their knowledge. We also get a glimpse of that mysterious and inextinguishable fire that burned in the breast of men such as Magellan and Columbus—the fire that has propelled all those throughout the ages who have been driven to leave behind family and friends for a voyage into the unknown.

No one has ever satisfactorily explained the urge to explore, the drive to go to the "back of beyond." It is certain that it has been present in man almost since he began walking erect and first ventured across the African savannas. Sparks from that same fire fueled the transoceanic explorers of the Ice Age, who led their people across the vast plain that formed a land bridge between Asia and North America, and the astronauts and scientists who determined that man must reach the moon.

Besides an element of adventure, all exploration involves an element of mystery. We must not confuse exploration with discovery. Exploration is a purposeful human activity—a search for something. Discovery may be the end result of that search; it may also be an accident, as when Columbus found a whole new world while searching for the Indies. Often, the explorer may not even realize the full significance of what he has discovered, as was the case with Columbus. Exploration, on the other hand, is the product of a cultural or individual curiosity; it is a unique process that has enabled mankind to know and understand the world's oceans, continents, and polar regions. It is at the heart of scientific thinking. One of its most significant aspects is that it teaches people to ask the right questions; by doing so, it forces us to reevaluate what we think we know and understand. Thus knowledge progresses, and we are driven constantly to a new awareness and appreciation of the universe in all its infinite variety.

The motivation for exploration is not always pure. In his fascination with the new, man often forgets that others have been there before him. For example, the popular notion of the discovery of America overlooks the complex Indian civilizations that had existed there for thousands of years before the arrival of Europeans. Man's desire for conquest, riches, and fame is often linked inextricably with his quest for the unknown, but a story that touches so closely on the human essence must of necessity treat war as well as peace, avarice with generosity, both pride and humility, frailty and greatness. The story of exploration is above all a story of humanity and of man's understanding of his place in the universe.

The WORLD EXPLORERS series has been divided into four sections. The first treats the explorers of the ancient world, the Viking explorers of the 9th through the 11th centuries, and Marco Polo and the medieval explorers. The rest of the series is divided into three great ages of exploration. The first is the era of Columbus and Magellan: the period spanning the 15th and 16th centuries, which saw the discovery and exploration of the New World and the world ocean. The second might be called the age of science and imperialism, the era made possible by the scientific advances of the 17th century, which witnessed the discovery of the world's last two undiscovered continents, Australia and Antarctica, the mapping of all the continents and oceans, and the establishment of colonies all over the world. The third great age refers to the most ambitious quests of the 20th century—the probing of space and of the ocean's depths.

As we reach out into the darkness of outer space and other galaxies, we come to better understand how our ancestors confronted *oecumene,* or the vast earthly unknown. We learn once again the meaning of an unknown 18th-century sea captain's advice to navigators:

> And if by chance you make a landfall on the shores of another sea in a far country inhabited by savages and barbarians, remember you this: the greatest danger and the surest hope lies not with fires and arrows but in the quicksilver hearts of men.

At its core, exploration is a series of moral dramas. But it is these dramas, involving new lands, new people, and exotic ecosystems of staggering beauty, that make the explorers' stories not only moral tales but also some of the greatest adventure stories ever recorded. They represent the process of learning in its most expansive and vivid forms. We see that real life, past and present, transcends even the adventures of the starship *Enterprise.*

A Trip into the Unknown

The object of your mission is to explore the Missouri river,
& such principal stream[s] of it, as, by it's course and
communication with the waters of the Pacific ocean . . .
may offer the most direct & practicable water
communication across this continent.
                    —Thomas Jefferson to Meriwether Lewis,
                                            June 20, 1803

An expedition into the western lands of North America
was born in the mind of Thomas Jefferson long before he
became the third president of the United States and
launched Meriwether Lewis and William Clark up the
Missouri and into history in the spring of 1804. Jefferson
had dreamed of such an expedition for at least 20 years
before the Louisiana Purchase and during that period had
attempted to initiate it several times. First, in 1783, he
tried to induce George Rogers Clark, the frontiersman hero
of the revolutionary war and older brother of William, to
undertake the mission. Ten years later, he sponsored an
abortive effort by the renowned French botanist André
Michaux "to seek for & pursue that route which shall form
the shortest & most convenient communication between
the higher parts of the Missouri & the Pacific ocean." The
words in quotations are Jefferson's, and it is interesting to
note how closely they resemble the instructions he gave
Meriwether Lewis on the eve of his journey.

John Wesley Jarvis's portrait of a young Meriwether Lewis, probably from the time Lewis served as secretary to his fellow Virginian, President Thomas Jefferson. The Jarvis portrait is one of the few existing likenesses of Lewis as a young man done from life.

But political complications involving the relationship between the young United States and revolutionary France sabotaged Michaux's journey, and Jefferson was unable to further act on his interest in western exploration until after assuming the presidency in 1801. As president, Jefferson had several pressing reasons for concerning himself with the western lands. In early 1802, he read Alexander Mackenzie's two-volume account of his transcontinental crossing of Canada, *Voyages from Montreal, on the River St. Lawrence Through the Continent of North America, to the Frozen and Pacific Oceans; in the years 1789 and 1793.* In 1792–93, Mackenzie, a young fur trapper and partner

National political and economic concerns partially motivated Jefferson's interest in exploring the western lands, but the greatest impetus was his thirst for knowledge. From his youth, Jefferson had been greatly interested in the American frontier.

in the North West Fur Company, journeyed from Lake Athabasca (which spans the present-day border of Alberta and Saskatchewan) via the Peace, Fraser, and Bella Coola rivers and countless portages across the Rocky Mountains and all the way to the Pacific Ocean. There, in vermilion letters, he proudly inscribed on a rock: "Alexander Mackenzie, from Canada, by land, the twenty-second of July, one thousand seven hundred and ninety-three." His account of his journey is a classic of wilderness exploration. It fired Jefferson's imagination, but it also left the president uneasy, for in becoming the first man to cross the continent, Mackenzie, a British subject, had seemingly furthered his nation's claim to the Northwest as well as opened new routes for the fur trade.

Not long afterward, Jefferson was presented with the opportunity to purchase from France the Louisiana Territory, a huge expanse of land reaching as far north from the Gulf of Mexico as the upper part of present-day Montana and as far west from the Mississippi River as the border of present-day Montana and Idaho. Although the Constitution did not explicitly authorize the president to make such a purchase, Jefferson went ahead with the deal. At a total cost of $15 million, the buy worked out to about 3 cents an acre. The Louisiana Purchase, which encompassed all or part of 15 future states, more than doubled the territory of the young republic.

Now, more than ever, Jefferson had both reason and opportunity to pursue his dream of westward exploration. The territory immediately beyond the Mississippi and far westward was now U.S. and not foreign property, which removed one major impediment to American exploration. Recognizing that in the future the United States would inevitably expand beyond the Mississippi, Jefferson was determined to find out all he could about the new territory—its geographical features; the length and location of its waterways; its suitability for human habitation and economic and agricultural development; the location and number of its Indian tribes; possible sites for forts and trading posts to protect future settlers, cement the United States's claim to the region, and possibly divert the fur trade south from various Canadian outposts; and, most important, whether an easily traversed water route connected the Mississippi River with the Pacific Ocean.

Jefferson's choice of Meriwether Lewis to head this important mission grew out of confidence formed from a lifelong acquaintance. Lewis was born on August 18, 1774, at his family's plantation, Locust Hill, in Albemarle County, Virginia, a short distance from Jefferson's home, Monticello. His first name, which sounds somewhat unusual to modern ears, was his mother Lucy's maiden name. After the death of Lewis's father, William, in November 1779 and his mother's remarriage to John Marks, the family moved to Georgia, but they returned to Locust Hill after Lucy was widowed once more in 1792. During his youth Lewis received only a rudimentary education, but he developed a keen interest in natural history, whetted by his exploratory hikes in the Virginia countryside.

Like others of his generation, he found his first calling in military service—for young Lewis, militia duty during the Whiskey Rebellion in 1794. Within a year he joined the regular army as ensign, the equivalent to a modern lieutenant, and the next year was transferred to the First Infantry Regiment. By 1800, he had risen to the rank of captain. During these years he moved about on various assignments, seeing no combat but gaining experience at command, frontier living, and dealing with Indians. It was also during this period, at Fort Greenville, Ohio, that he met William Clark, a fellow Virginian four years his senior who was his superior officer for a time. Little is known of that encounter except that that they struck a deep friendship that lasted their lifetimes.

Jefferson called Lewis from military duty to become his private secretary shortly after being elected to the presidency. Despite his new duties, Lewis was allowed to retain his army rank. Recent historical research indicates that Jefferson may have selected the young officer not only to groom him for western exploration but also to use Lewis's knowledge of military personnel in order to evaluate officers appointed by the Federalist party, Jefferson's political rivals. But by 1802, it is clear, Jefferson was already preparing Lewis to head a westward expedition. Lewis often accompanied the president to his home at Monticello, where Jefferson encouraged him to make use of his magnificent personal library in order to inform himself on the many subjects he would need to know—botany, medicine, natural history, navigation and astronomy, geology, mineralogy, meteorology, cartography, anthropology, Indian affairs, foreign relations. One may also assume that Jefferson lectured his young protégé in order to provide him with his own considerable insight on these topics.

What Jefferson wanted for a western expedition, he confided to a friend, was a person "perfectly skilled in botany, natural history, mineralogy, astronomy, with at the same time the necessary firmness of body & mind, habits of living in the woods & familiarity with the Indian character." He knew that no such person existed but that Lewis filled the latter requirements perfectly and could be sufficiently trained in the former to carry out his duties in the field. With that in mind he sent Lewis to study with some of the young republic's leading scientists.

Lewis set out from Washington in the middle of March 1803, first for the federal armory at Harpers Ferry, Virginia, where he purchased some weapons for the planned expedition, including rifles, pistols, tomahawks, and knives. The 15 rifles he ordered were prototypes or predecessors of the new standard army weapon then under development, the Harpers Ferry Model 1803, the first weapon designed specifically for the U.S. Army. Lewis also oversaw the construction of a portable iron-frame boat of his own design, which he intended to pack across the continent, unload on the upper reaches of the Missouri,

(continued on page 20)

Alexander Mackenzie and his party of nine men were the first whites to cross North America. Historian William H. Goetzmann has described Mackenzie's book on his travels as "perhaps the most influential North American explorer's account ever published." It directly influenced Jefferson's decision to send his own expedition west.

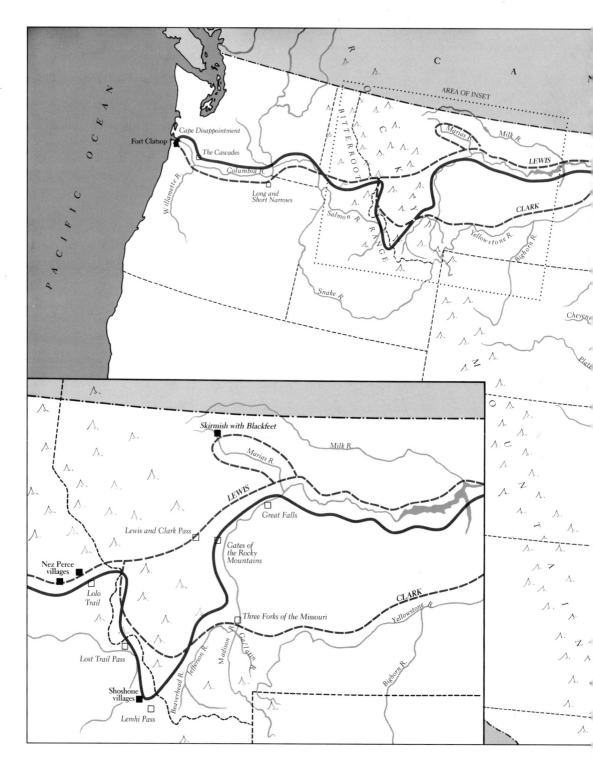

PACIFIC OCEAN

Cape Disappointment
Fort Clatsop
The Cascades
Willamette R.
Columbia R.
Long and
Short Narrows

BITTERROOT RANGE

ROCKY

AREA OF INSET

Marias R.   Milk R.

LEWIS

CLARK

Salmon R.

Yellowstone R.

Bighorn R.

Snake R.

Cheyen

MO

Platt

Skirmish with Blackfeet

Milk R.

Marias R.

LEWIS

Great Falls

Lewis and Clark Pass

Gates of
the Rocky
Mountains

CLARK

Nez Perce
villages

Yellowstone R.

Lolo
Trail

Three Forks of the Missouri

Beaverhead R.

Jefferson R.

Madison R.

Gallatin R.

Bighorn R.

Lost Trail Pass

Shoshone
villages

Lemhi Pass

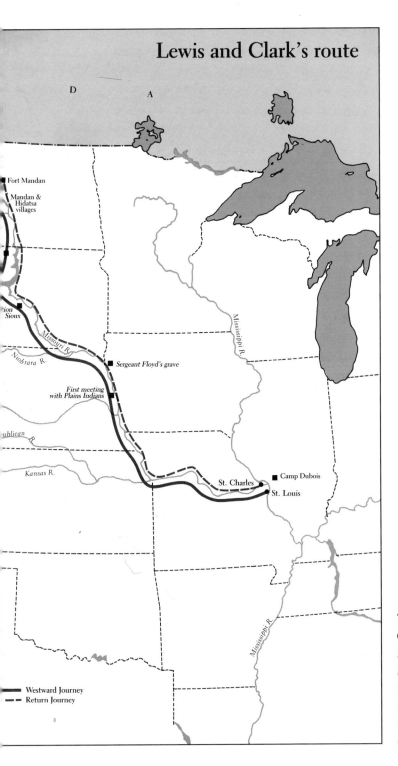

Lewis and Clark's route

D   A

Fort Mandan

Mandan &
Hidatsa
villages

Missouri R.

ion
Sioux

Niobrara R.

Mississippi R.

Sergeant Floyd's grave

First meeting
with Plains Indians

ublican R.

Kansas R.

Camp Dubois

St. Charles

St. Louis

Mississippi R.

— Westward Journey
-- Return Journey

The route taken by Lewis and Clark on their way west and back. The Voyage of Discovery lasted 28 months, covered more than 8,000 miles, and was the best-managed expedition in the history of North American exploration.

19

The eminent Philadelphia physician Benjamin Rush was among the scientific experts Lewis consulted in preparation for the expedition. A signer of the Declaration of Independence, Rush had stirred much controversy during Philadelphia's great epidemics of the 1790s for his advocacy of bleeding as the most effective treatment for patients afflicted with yellow fever.

(continued from page 17)

and navigate through shallow waters. Weighing only 44 pounds, it could theoretically accommodate a load of more than 1,700 pounds.

After about a month at Harpers Ferry, Lewis continued on to Lancaster, Pennsylvania, in order to visit astronomer Andrew Ellicott. Ellicott taught Lewis to "shoot the stars" so that he could locate his position in the unknown lands. He also received additional training from Robert Patterson, professor of mathematics at the University of Pennsylvania, when he moved on to Philadelphia, where he spent the entire month of May. There, he picked up additional instruction in the sciences from friends of Jefferson who, like the president, were members of the American Philosophical Society, the nation's foremost learned society. Benjamin Rush, the country's most eminent physician, recommended medical supplies and gave advice on health care. From Benjamin Smith Barton, professor of botany at the University of Pennsylvania, Lewis probably received instruction in botanical and zoological identification, classification, and preservation. Further help came from Caspar Wistar, professor of anatomy and the leading American authority on fossils. Lewis also got a smattering of training in classifying plants and animals under the comparatively new system, devised by Carolus Linnaeus of Sweden, that over time would become the basis for all scientific classification. Nevertheless, Lewis only rarely categorized species under the Linnaean system in his journals.

Lewis had also come to Philadelphia to outfit the expedition, and he arrived with a shopping list in hand. It was primarily a guide to purchases, and Lewis altered its contents after conversations with consultants and local merchants. The captain's scientific requisitions included artificial horizons, octants, quadrants, sextants, and compasses—the most modern astronomical, navigational, and surveying instruments available. An experienced soldier, Lewis knew what camp equipment was needed, so he loaded up on tents, tools, and cooking utensils. He also added four tin horns, to be sounded in order to call the expedition's soldiers together. Finally, he purchased 193 pounds of "portable soup," sealed in 32 canisters—19th-century field rations. Food, however, was of a lesser priority than many other items, for it was fully expected that the Corps of Discovery, as the men of the expedition were to be known, would live off the land by hunting and fishing.

Lewis filled his medical stores under the tutelage of Rush. He procured 600 of the doctor's famous bilious pills, a powerful and fast-acting laxative known humorously as "Rush's thunderbolts." His medical chest included quinine, diuretics, laudanum, poultices, astringents, and emetics. Lewis also expected to make use of natural medicines, gathered along the route from bushes or shrubs. His mother, Lucy, a well-known herbalist, had doubtless schooled her son in the use of medicinal plants, and Jefferson had instructed Lewis to learn what he could of Indian methods of treatment of disease. A few basic surgical instruments were also included among the expedition's provisions.

Finally, the captain procured a list of goods that fell under the general heading "Indian presents." Presenting gifts to Indian dignitaries was a time-honored tradition, one that the Indians had come to expect, and no diplomatic transaction was complete without such an offering. The most impressive of the gifts were the Indian peace medals. Made of silver, varying in size, they bore on one side the likeness of the president and on the reverse an engraving of clasped hands, a crossed tomahawk and peace

A replica of one of the peace medals Jefferson ordered coined for distribution by Lewis and Clark to Indian chiefs on the Voyage of Discovery. The other side bore a likeness of Jefferson. The medals were used by some Indian chiefs as passports when they accepted the captains' offer to visit Jefferson in Washington, D.C.

pipe, and the words *peace and friendship*. The presents, which aside from the peace medals included brightly colored ribbons and cloth, glass and pewter beads, fishhooks, knives, small mirrors, combs, and tobacco, were also intended as a medium of exchange. When the party's food ran low or game was difficult to find, the explorers planned on using their stock of trade goods to obtain provisions from the Indians. It was also intended that these goods be used to whet the Indians' appetites for future trade with the Americans rather than with the British, French, or Spanish.

Before leaving Philadelphia, Lewis made arrangements to have his supplies transported to Pittsburgh, the city on the Ohio River that was to serve as his jumping-off point to the west, as he had done with the goods from Harpers Ferry. He left the city the first week in June, heading back to Washington for final instructions from Jefferson and for the important task of securing a partner in command.

As conceived by Jefferson, the expedition was the first government-sponsored scientific enterprise of the United States. It was to reflect all of the president's and the nation's myriad interests, but the true purpose of the endeavor was scientific inquiry, and to that end Jefferson instructed Lewis carefully. In a detailed letter written in June 1803, the president outlined his intentions for the expedition.

The most important part of the president's instructions concerned geographical discovery, both for the sake of knowledge itself and for the promotion of future American development. The explorers were to attempt to find a relatively easy passage from the headwaters of the Missouri to a major tributary of the Columbia, which was known to empty into the Pacific Ocean. Their scientific work in this area would include taking observations of longitude and latitude, noting significant geographic features, and making detailed route maps.

Moreover, Jefferson desired investigations into what is now called ecology. Such studies, Jefferson instructed his protégé, would include reports on plant and animal life, mineral deposits, and the climate of the new country. The intent was both to increase knowledge and to evaluate the prospects of these regions for future settlement and agricultural development. Accordingly, Lewis and Clark's journals of the expedition are filled with notes not only on new plant and animal species but also on the seasonal changes and range of plant life, of the range and behavior of animals, and of the migrations of birds and mammals. The explorers also noted geological features and possible mineral deposits, and they developed tables for daily weather observations that included comments on noteworthy climatic occurrences.

The president's lengthiest instructions to Lewis, however, concerned the Indians. His words to the young man sound like a teacher's charge to a star pupil, for the captain was to learn the names, numbers, and locations of the Indian tribes inhabiting the region, their intertribal relations, trading patterns, languages, occupations, food, clothing, health, types of shelter, traditions, laws, customs, morality, and religion. Above all, Jefferson insisted, the Corps must maintain good personal relations to ensure its own safety and success, for "in the loss of yourselves, we should lose also the information you will have acquired." Lewis was to take pains to convince the Indians of the goodwill of the United States and of the desire of the young republic to enter into mutually beneficial trade relations. He was also to encourage their chiefs to visit Washington, D.C., at the public expense, so as to inform themselves firsthand of the power, wealth, and generosity of the new inheritor of the western territory.

In their studies of Indian culture, Lewis and Clark would be handicapped, as were most of their contemporaries, by prejudices and preconceptions about the natives. As the science of anthropology was in its infancy, the explorers lacked training now taken for granted. Nonetheless, they provided their contemporaries with the first detailed descriptions of three major Indian groups: the village Indians of the upper Missouri; the intermountain tribes of the northern Rocky Mountains; and the peoples of the lower Columbia River and the Northwest Coast. Hampered as they were by language barriers and lack of time, the explorers were unable to gain a deep understanding of these peoples, yet they still displayed a degree of objectivity unusual for their time.

A Blackfoot Indian on horseback. The Blackfeet lived north of the Missouri and like other northern tribes traded with Canadian fur traders. Jefferson told Congress that one of the purposes of the expedition was to explore possible future sites for trading posts that would divert this fur trade south.

During the return trip from Philadelphia to Washington to meet with Jefferson, Lewis had taken the time to ask his friend and former colleague, William Clark, to join him as co-commander of the expedition "in it's fatiegues, it's dangers and it's honors." (For all their virtues, neither man excelled in spelling, grammar, or punctuation; it is a testimony to the power of expression of both, and to the sheer magnitude of the expedition, that the journals make such compelling reading nonetheless.) Delays in the mail caused Lewis some frustration on this point, to the extent that he even invited another officer, Lieutenant Moses Hooke, to accompany him in case Clark declined. He need not have worried; although his answer was slow in arriving, Clark had replied enthusiastically the day after getting Lewis's letter, writing that "no man lives whith whome I would perfur to undertake Such a Trip."

The red-haired Clark was born in Caroline County, Virginia, on August 1, 1770. He was the sixth son and ninth of 10 children; his 5 older brothers, including the famed George Rogers Clark, all distinguished themselves on the American side in the revolutionary war. Apparently, Jefferson did not know the younger Clark but was well acquainted with his family, even though he consistently spelled the name "Clarke." When Clark was 14, the family moved to the site of today's Louisville, Kentucky, which was then on the westernmost edge of the American frontier. From there, he enlisted in the militia and transferred to the regular army in 1791. His fine performance in campaigns against the Indians in the Ohio Valley enabled him to rise to the rank of captain, and in his capacity as commander of a rifle unit at Fort Greenville, Ohio, he made the acquaintance of a talented junior officer named Meriwether Lewis. Family problems forced Clark to resign his military commission and return home to Kentucky in 1796. In the years between his resignation and Lewis's offer, he had maintained the family property near Louisville and with his brother George had farmed a new claim across the Ohio at present-day Clarksville, Indiana.

A potential snafu arose when a mix-up in the army bureaucracy in Washington denied Clark the captain's rank that Lewis had promised him. An aggravated Lewis told Clark that his "grade has no effect upon your compensation, which G—d, shall be equal to my own." The leaders hid the matter of Clark's lower rank from their men and throughout the trip shared the command equally, and during the expedition Clark occasionally signed himself as captain of a Corps of Discovery.

Writers have tended to emphasize and even exaggerate the apparent differences in the characters of the two men. Lewis is usually cast as the moody, sensitive intellectual, with a pronounced strain of melancholia, Clark as the pragmatic, outgoing, and less literate frontiersman. Although there is some validity to such a comparison, the contrasts are often overstated. What is much more important is the extraordinary degree of cooperation that existed between the two men. They complemented each other exceptionally well, and in the 28 months of the expedition, there was no hint of disagreement between them. It is inconceivable to think that the expedition could have fared as well as it did without the services of either man. Each regarded the other with the greatest of respect and affection. Clark even named his firstborn son Meriwether Lewis Clark.

As the party's naturalist and astronomer, Lewis performed most of the expedition's scientific tasks, and he was often absent from the party on intellectual quests. His writing is more technical than Clark's, with more of a literary flair, and he was a more talented and precise observer of flora and fauna. Clark worked primarily as the party's engineer, and his writing tends to be more matter-of-fact. His eccentric spelling, grammar, and punctuation, resulting from a lack of formal education and the loose rules of that era, have accentuated his reputation as a

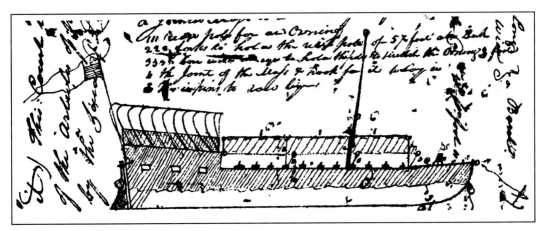

Clark drew this sketch of the keelboat that carried the Corps of Discovery up the Missouri to the Mandan villages. The boat was about 55 feet in length, had an extremely shallow draft, and could be sailed, rowed, poled, or towed along.

backwoodsman, yet his vocabulary and phrasing are hardly those of an illiterate man. As an officer, landowner, and public official, he would have been considered a gentleman in most circles of American society, and he would have resented being classed with the rougher sort of frontiersmen.

After leaving Washington on July 5, Lewis crossed the Appalachian Mountains to Pittsburgh and there supervised the construction of the 55-foot keelboat that was to carry the majority of the Corps of Discovery and its provisions up the Missouri. The boat was designed to carry 10 tons in cargo yet maintain a shallow draft. It had a mast to support a square sail, a cabin in the rear, and walkways on either side, plus plenty of storage room throughout.

Lewis was eager to make a quick start, but he found himself frustrated in his attempts to leave Pittsburgh and link up with Clark. Construction of the keelboat was delayed repeatedly, apparently because, as Lewis complained, the workmen were "incorrigible drunkards." During the wait Lewis purchased a pirogue—a flat-bottomed, dugout "canoe," as he described it, widely used on the western waters. This canoe was considerably larger than the crafts one usually thinks of in connection with that term; hewn from the trunk of tree, it probably measured close to 50 feet in length, with a mast and a sail.

At Pittsburgh, Lewis also bought, for $20, his large New-foundland dog, Seaman.

With the keelboat at last finished and the Ohio River at sufficient depth to carry him forward, Lewis set out at 11:00 on the morning of August 31, 1803. That day, he made his first entry in a small leather-bound notebook. In it and numerous other journals, the captains and four enlisted men would fill hundreds of pages with more than a million words, a priceless record of events, observation , and impressions of the new lands. An invaluable literary and scientific legacy, the journals are also replete with high drama; tense encounters with natives; dangerous river crossings and precipitous mountain traverses; hunger, thirst, and bodily fatigue; the tedium of daily routine and of simple hard work.

Impeded by low water, Lewis did not arrive in Clarks-ville, where Clark awaited him, until about October 15. There, several recruits signed on, chiefly young Kentucky woodsmen enlisted by Clark. York, Clark's black slave, also became a member of the party. The party left Clarks-ville on October 26 and proceeded down the Ohio, reach-ing its confluence with the Mississippi in mid-November. After a week spent mapping and measuring and taking celestial observations, they started up the Mississippi on November 20. On their left was present-day Missouri, part of the Louisiana Purchase, still directed by Spanish offi-cials pending its imminent transfer to the United States, and on the right, modern-day Illinois, American territory. On November 28, Lewis left Clark in charge of the men and went by land to St. Louis to confer with Spanish authorities. (France had obtained the Louisiana Territory from Spain, but had owned it for so brief a time that Spain had not yet removed its officials before the region was sold to the United States.) As Clark moved on upriver looking for the best spot to establish a winter camp, returning hunters reported that the country was beautiful in every direction and teeming with game.

A Winter of Preparation

> My situation is as comfortable as could be expected in the woods; . . . The Missouri which mouths imedeately opposet is the river we intend assending as soon as the weather will permit. . . . We are collecting what information we can of this river and its rises so as we may make just Calculations, before we set out.
> —William Clark to William Croghan, January 15, 1804

After working the boats up the Mississippi against a hard wind on December 12, Clark arrived at about two o'clock in the afternoon at the mouth of a small river coming in from the northeast. The next day, on the south side of this stream, in present-day Illinois, he established his camp. For the next five months this spot would serve as winter quarters for the Corps of Discovery. Located directly across from the mouth of the Missouri, the little river was then called Rivière à Dubois, after some long forgotten Frenchman whose name translates as Wood.

Long usage has since rendered the stream's name as Wood River and the party's encampment as Camp Dubois or Camp Wood. Here, the captains selected and disciplined their troops and molded a disparate group of men into the Corps of Discovery, which would conquer the continent. They also began to sharpen their skills at the many tasks they would have to perform over the next 28 months. They made their initial efforts at scientific descriptions and astronomical observations, tested and retested their equipment, visited with Indians, gathered

William Clark, as portrayed by the Philadelphia painter Charles Willson Peale, whose museum would eventually house many of the specimens obtained in the West by the Corps of Discovery. Like his counterpart Lewis, Clark was a muscular six-footer, but his most prominent physical characteristic was his red hair.

advice from seasoned river travelers, and recorded events in rough journal notes. Camp Dubois can fittingly be called the proving ground of the Lewis and Clark expedition.

Clark quickly put his men to clearing the area of timber and to cutting logs for huts and a stockade; within three days, cabins were rising. The buildings were nearly complete by December 20, but Clark was not able to move into his for another 10 days, by which time rain, sleet, and snow had been falling for more than a week and ice ran thick in the Mississippi. Crude sketches in Clark's field notes show the general layout of the fortification. Roughly rectangular in shape, the structure had four cabins for the enlisted men, one at each corner of the exterior. In the center of the enclosed grounds were three additional cabins for storage and for officers' quarters. Despite the cold and drizzly weather that winter the men remained dry, warm, and comfortable in the woods. On clear days some even moved outside into their tents.

During the 5 months at Camp Dubois the captains gathered more recruits to add to the men who had come down the Ohio with them. Originally, plans called for a contingent of only 10 to 12 men, but more mature con-

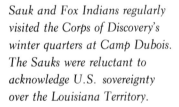

Sauk and Fox Indians regularly visited the Corps of Discovery's winter quarters at Camp Dubois. The Sauks were reluctant to acknowledge U.S. sovereignty over the Louisiana Territory.

sideration decided that a much greater force was needed in order to move the heavy keelboat and pirogues upriver and provide security against Indian attack. The hope was that a show of numbers would discourage belligerence on the part of the Indians. The long and inevitably tedious winter enabled the captains to evaluate their men, to weed out a few undesirables, and to introduce the more undisciplined to the rigors of army regimen. Those not already in the regular army had to enlist as soldiers.

Lewis and Clark gathered their troops from frontiersmen in the Ohio Valley, from enlisted men at regional military posts, and from French boatmen in the neighborhood of St. Louis. Lewis began recruiting as early as his stay in Pittsburgh. He was looking, he said then, for "good hunters, stout, healthy, unmarried men, accustomed to the woods, and capable of bearing bodily fatigue in a pretty considerable degree." It is not certain, however, which members of the party he signed up at that point, and it is probable that he enlisted several individuals who did not become members of the Corps of Discovery.

Clark was directed by Lewis to choose capable young backwoodsmen in Indiana and Kentucky. His enlistees have become known as the "nine young men from Kentucky"—William E. Bratton, John Colter, the brothers Reuben and Joseph Field, Charles Floyd, George Gibson, Nathaniel Pryor, George Shannon, and John Shields. However, Colter and Shannon may actually have joined Lewis earlier at Maysville, Kentucky. The nine are some of the most noteworthy members of the expedition. Colter later achieved fame for his exploits as a fur trader and trapper in the Rockies and is remembered as one of the first and greatest of that hardy, solitary breed known as the mountain men. The Field brothers were involved in nearly every special assignment and difficult task, and they are mentioned repeatedly in the captains' journals. Floyd and Pryor were cousins and were expedition sergeants; Floyd's ancestors had been among the first settlers of Kentucky.

Shannon was the youngest member of the party, while Shields, the only married man, was particularly valuable as a blacksmith.

The other members of the expedition evidently signed on during the winter at Wood River. Some were soldiers from nearby army posts, Fort Massac and Fort Kaskaskia in Illinois. Among them was John Ordway, who retained his rank and served the unit as top sergeant at Camp Dubois. Ordway may have been accompanied by Patrick Gass, who was later elected sergeant and has the distinction of being the first to publish an account of the expedition.

In December eight enlistees arrived from a post at South West Point, near present-day Knoxville, Tennessee. Four of them were apparently unsuitable and were dismissed. Among those who were allowed to stay was Corporal Richard Warfington, who would lead a detachment back from North Dakota after the first winter. It appears that some of the men detached to Lewis and Clark from regional military posts may have been unwanted by their superiors. Such unloading of undesirables may account for some of the unruliness at Camp Dubois, where episodes of drunkenness and brawling occasionally occurred. Other recruits included George Drouillard, whose French Canadian name the captains never got right and usually spelled as "Drewyer." The son of a French Canadian father and a Shawnee mother, Drouillard would also achieve fame as a mountain man. He and York were the only two non-military men to complete the entire expedition. Drouillard signed on as a civilian interpreter and hunter for a salary of $25 per month; his ability with a rifle and his skill with the sign language used by the Plains Indians made him one of the most valuable members of the Corps.

In all, the Corps of Discovery at Camp Dubois apparently totaled about 40 men, counting some French hired hands whose number is uncertain. In their minds Lewis and Clark always separated the men into two groups: those of the permanent party who would travel the full route, and those on temporary assignment to the first wintering post. The latter group would return the unwieldy keelboat to St. Louis and carry dispatches for Jefferson. By April 1, 1804, the officers had determined the makeup of the two parties. Some adjustments were made during the expedition, however, as additional persons were taken on and others were replaced. The permanent party at this time consisted of the 2 captains, 3 sergeants, 26 enlisted men, York, and Drouillard. The remaining men, to be led by Warfington, constituted the temporary hands.

About most of these men there exists only the barest of information. Most lived obscure lives before and after their season of glory with Lewis and Clark. Some, such as Colter and Drouillard, achieved distinction apart from the expedition, and others, like the Field brothers, come alive in the pages of the captains' diaries. But many others received no more than casual mention in the journals and are completely lost to us. The men represented diverse origins and backgrounds and came from many states: from Kentucky, Indiana, and Virginia, of course, but also from Connecticut, Maryland, Massachusetts, New Hampshire, North Carolina, Pennsylvania, and Vermont. One, John Potts, was born in Germany. Whatever their role, they all shared in the toils of the expedition, and they share as well in its renown.

Although they alternated, for most of the winter Clark maintained command at Camp Dubois while Lewis pursued information about the western lands from knowledgeable sources in nearby St. Louis. Clark's notes about the daily routine of activities at the camp are quite meager. Although there is no record of his drilling the men in field or on parade, one can assume that the men carried out the usual duties of frontier soldiers, for Clark was a former regular army officer used to strict military procedures. The men spent much of the time hunting, checking equipment, packing and loading supplies, and refitting and repairing the boats.

The Frenchman René Auguste Chouteau was one of the founders of the city of St. Louis. Having become wealthy from the fur trade with the Osage Indians, he and his brother Jean Pierre were the leading lights of St. Louis society. The Chouteau brothers were extremely helpful in outfitting and preparing Lewis and Clark for the expedition.

*Front Street, along the
Mississippi in St. Louis. The
Chouteau brothers' warehouse
can be seen about midway down
the thoroughfare. Long an
outpost for French fur traders
along the Mississippi and the
Missouri, in the years following
the* Voyage of Discovery *St. Louis
would become the jumping-off
point for countless American
expeditions into the interior.*

Garrison life is generally hard on discipline. The Wood
River camp, with its monotonous daily routine, was no
exception. Virtually all of the men came in for some dis-
ciplinary action during the winter. Most of the infractions
had to do with drunkenness, fighting, or insubordination,
but were probably due as much to close quarters, boredom,
and pent-up, youthful energies. Rowdy frontier soldiers
traditionally tested their officers and strained at military
discipline. Some of those most often disciplined, such as
Colter and Reuben Field, proved in time to be among the
ablest and most reliable men of the Corps.

The countryside surrounding the camp abounded in
game, so the Corps' hunters were always out and active.
Almost any game was acceptable on a soldier's table;
grouse, turkey, and deer were standard mealtime fare, and
bear and raccoon were sometimes also taken. Staples such
as milk, butter, cheese, eggs, sugar, flour, meal, and veg-

etables were purchased from nearby settlers. Clark had the men clear a road to a nearby prairie so supplies could be brought in by wagon team. No one went hungry at Camp Dubois that winter.

The monotony of camp life was occasionally broken by visitors. People from nearby settlements came in for visits and sometimes engaged in shooting contests with the men. Clark was happy to report his men's abilities with their guns, but another time he had to say, "All git beet and Lose their money." Curious Indians also wandered into the camp—Kickapoo, Sauk, and Delaware. Passing boatmen also stopped by, and Clark no doubt quizzed them thoroughly about the Missouri's secrets.

Although Lewis took responsibility for most of the Corps' scientific duties, at Camp Dubois, Clark also attempted to take astronomical readings, and on January 1, 1804, he began systematically recording meteorological information in a separate journal to be used solely for that purpose. Throughout the expedition Lewis and Clark shared in this chore; most of the time duplicate records were maintained. The weather notebooks are quite extensive and include not only temperature readings taken twice daily but also descriptions of the state of the river, the direction of the wind, and general conditions, all on tables developed especially for that purpose.

Lewis spent most of his time in St. Louis or in nearby Cahokia or Kaskaskia talking with persons familiar with the Missouri River and the interior country. He also made occasional trips to Camp Dubois, but his most important work was gaining advice and information. His most useful St. Louis informants were fur traders, the brothers René Auguste and Jean Pierre Chouteau and their brother-in-law Charles Gratiot. Also helpful were Antoine Soulard, a Frenchman who served the Spanish as surveyor general, and John Hay, a Cahokia merchant familiar with the north country. Some information may also have been provided by the Spanish fur trader Manuel Lisa.

After the Chouteaus, Soulard, and Hay, Lewis's most useful information came from the work of James Mackay and John Thomas Evans, who had ascended the Missouri River together in 1795–97. Lewis was able to obtain copies of their maps and journal from the trip, and Mackay even visited Camp Dubois during the winter and may have met with Lewis in St. Louis. On their journey, Mackay had gotten as far as modern-day northern Nebraska, and Evans had continued on to the Mandan and Hidatsa Indian villages along the Missouri in what is today north central North Dakota. Evans completed a detailed set of maps of the river, showing all its bends and affluents, and Mackay later compiled this material into a master map of the river.

After collecting as much information as possible from maps, journals, and area informants, Lewis and Clark had a fairly accurate picture of the Missouri River's course up to the Mandan and Hidatsa villages. Indeed, the Mackay-Evans maps were nearly as good as those Clark would produce on the way up. The captain's cartography simply expanded on and confirmed the splendid work done by these earlier travelers. Moreover, the American officers had also gained fairly substantial information about the nature of the Indian tribes they would encounter. This sort of intelligence enabled Clark to make stunningly accurate estimates about the length of time the first leg of the journey would take, but the captains possessed much less accurate information for the immense spaces beyond the Mandan-Hidatsa villages. No one really knew how long it would take to get from the villages to the Rocky Mountains and then beyond to the Pacific Ocean. Clark hoped that after their winter in the wilderness, the Corps of Discovery would reach the coast in June or July 1805 and return back to St. Louis by November or December of the same year, an estimate that proved far too optimistic.

With the advent of spring, activity at the camp took on a new intensity. Afternoon temperatures climbed into the sixties, the men abandoned their cabins in favor of tents, and all hands readied themselves for the ascent of the Missouri. Trial runs were made up and down the Mississippi in ladened boats. As the anticipation grew, Clark's journal entries grew shorter, until finally, on the morning of departure, May 14, 1804, he penned simply, "fixing for a Start."

Frontiersmen and Indians look on as the representatives of the French government transfer the Louisiana Territory to the United States at St. Louis on March 10, 1804. Both Lewis and Clark attended the ceremony.

Under a Gentle Breeze

Honored Parence. I am now on an expidition to the westward, with Capt. Lewis and Capt. Clark. . . . We are to ascend the Missouri River with a boat as far as it is navigable and then to go by land, to the western ocean, if nothing prevents . . . and if we make Great Discoveries as we expect, the united states, has promised to make us Great Rewards.

> —John Ordway to his parents, April 8, 1804

I Set out at 4 oClock P.M. in the presence of many of the Neighbouring inhabitents, and proceeded on under a jentle brease up the Missouri.

> —William Clark, May 14, 1804

The morning of May 14, 1804, dawned cloudy and cool. Rain started to fall at nine o'clock, but by afternoon the temperature had climbed to the mid-sixties and the weather turned fair. At four o'clock, to the cheers of local settlers, the men fired the keelboat's swivel gun and set out, all in high spirits, according to Clark. Lewis was in St. Louis making final arrangements and would ride overland to meet them at St. Charles, a few miles up the river.

It is unclear how many men were with the expedition at the outset. The captains' apparent indifference to the number of temporary hands may explain discrepancies in the records. These Frenchmen, called *voyageurs* or *engagés* (engaged, or hired, men), were professional boatmen hired to pole and pull the heavy keelboat and two pirogues

Scavengers prowl around a burial scaffold of the Assiniboin Indians. Many of the northern tribes laid their dead to rest aboveground. Lewis and Clark never made direct contact with the Assiniboin, who were trading partners of the Mandan, the Hidatsa, and the Arikara, but the tribe played havoc with the captains' efforts at diplomacy by urging the Mandan and the Hidatsa not to enter into trade relations with the Americans.

Pawnee Indians watch from a bluff as travelers pass by on the plains below. The Pawnee were away on their seasonal buffalo hunt when the Voyage of Discovery passed through their territory. Although Lewis set the prairie on fire—a method commonly used by the Indians to summon another tribe to council—the Pawnee failed to show themselves.

up the Missouri as far as the first winter post. It appears that 42 men left Camp Dubois with Clark, organized into 3 squads of permanent soldiers and 2 units of temporary personnel; Drouillard had gone on ahead and, like Lewis, would catch up at St. Charles. The permanent party manned the keelboat for the most part, the French engagés took the larger, red pirogue, and the return detachment handled the smaller, white pirogue.

The party arrived at St. Charles on May 16. There, the loads in the boats were rearranged again, some last-minute supplies were purchased, and other final preparations were attended to. Extra boatmen were added, including the Frenchmen Pierre Cruzatte and François Labiche, who enlisted as privates in the permanent party. Both were of mixed blood, perhaps part Omaha Indian, so they could assist with interpreting Indian languages as well as translating French. Both were also expert Missouri boatmen.

Cruzatte is remembered for his fiddle playing, which greatly entertained soldiers and Indians alike, while Labiche took charge of the boats at several critical junctures.

Here, too, at St. Charles was the last chance for social pursuits among townspeople. The men entertained the villagers aboard the keelboat and were invited to parties in return. Some of the men went too far in their carousing, so that Clark called a court-martial and charged three of the men for misbehavior. On May 20, a Sunday, about 20 of the more sober celebrants attended mass. Lewis arrived that same evening; the next afternoon the men set out, again to the cheers of townsfolk lining the banks. Two days later they reached the little village of Femme Osage; Daniel Boone lived nearby, but there is no record of an encounter with the explorer. On May 26, the expedition passed the tiny cluster of cabins that constituted La Charette, the last white settlement on the river. Ahead lay the wilderness.

The journey up the Missouri, against the swift current, was slow and laborious. Occasionally the men raised the keelboat's sail under a favorable wind, but more often they poled or rowed their ungainly crafts or pulled the boats from the shore with a towrope. The Missouri's dark waters—the river carries so much sediment on its journey from the Rockies that it is often referred to as the Big Muddy—disguised many potential hazards, such as the type of snag the Frenchmen called an *embarras*, massive logs of driftwood entangled in the branches of toppled trees. Equally dangerous, if not more so, were sawyers—upended trees whose roots became embedded in the river bottom. The body of the tree bent with the powerful current until finally the roots gave way and the tree rocketed to the surface with tremendous force, like some arboreal torpedo. The men toiled in the stifling summer heat, pulling on their oars against the great river, crashing through the thick brush on shore with the towrope blistering their shoulders. Although the passage was tedious and slow, the land was lush and beautiful, and deer, elk, and bear abounded in the woods of walnut, ash, sycamore, linden, and cottonwood that lined the river. Clark, despite noting that "the party is much afflicted with *Boils*, and several have the Deasentary [dysentery]" and that the "Ticks and Musquiters are verry troublesome," reported no lack of high spirits and enthusiasm.

The party reached the mouth of the Kansas River, the future site of Kansas City, on June 26, and on July 21 passed the Platte River, in present-day Nebraska. The Corps was now 642 miles up the Missouri, by its own reckoning, averaging about 10 miles a day. At this point, at a site not far south of today's Council Bluffs, Iowa, the captains decided to call a halt to the expedition for several days in order to let the men rest, dry out wet gear, take celestial readings, and update their maps and journals. They also hoped to arrange a council with the local Indians, but the Oto and Pawnee were away on their buffalo hunt. The captains named the site of their rest stop Camp White Catfish, after a fish caught by one of the men.

By the afternoon of July 27 the Corps was on the move again. Three days later, the party made camp at the foot of a tall bluff. After climbing up the bank, Lewis and Clark were treated to the "most butifull prospect of the River up & Down . . . which I ever beheld." In the distance, the "Countrey" became "one continued Plain as fur as Can be seen" covered with "Grass of 10 or 12 inches in hight" and "Soil of good quality." In the meantime, one of the Frenchmen, La Liberté, was sent to see if he could locate some Indians and invite them to a council. The Indians arrived on August 2 and a successful parley was held. Speaking through an interpreter, Lewis told the Missouri and Oto in attendance that the United States now controlled the western lands and that they desired to have the Indians as their friends and trading partners. Gifts, including blue blankets, a bottle of whiskey, and the peace medals, were passed out, and Lewis demonstrated some of the marvels he had brought to amaze the Indians—magnetic compasses, magnifying glasses, and an air gun. Two days later, the conference broke up, and the Corps moved on, minus Private Moses B. Reed, who obtained permission to return downriver to retrieve a lost knife.

Several days later, neither La Liberté nor Reed had returned. When an investigation of Reed's knapsack revealed that he had taken his extra clothes and ammunition with him, the captains decided that he had probably deserted and sent out a search party, headed by Drouillard, to bring him in. Such breaches of discipline could not be allowed. Even a single desertion could set a bad example and encourage further such actions, which might in turn jeopardize the safety of all the members of the Corps and the very success of the expedition. On August 18, the search party returned, with Reed and three Oto chiefs. (La Liberté had been briefly apprehended, but he managed to escape; because he was a hired hand and not a member of the army, his offense was not considered as grave.) As the chiefs watched, Reed was tried, convicted, and expelled from the Corps of Discovery. He was also forced to run four times through a gauntlet composed of all the men of the expedition, each brandishing nine willow switches. The flogging appalled the chiefs, but they ceased their protests after Clark explained Reed's offense and that the punishment was one of "the Customs of our Countrey." (Legally, Reed's commanding officers could have

Prairie dogs are among the many specimens of wildlife that Lewis and Clark are credited with discovering. The captains were fascinated by the connecting burrows in which the "barking squirrels" lived. After lugging bucketfuls of water from the Missouri to pour down the burrows, they finally succeeded in capturing one.

Coyotes, as depicted by the great American naturalist John James Audubon. Lewis described the "prairie wolf" as being "of an intermediate size between that of the fox and dog, very active fleet and delicately formed. . . . They are of a pale redish brown colour. the eye of a deep sea green colour small and piercing."

had him shot.) Because it would have been virtually a death sentence to cut Reed loose on his own in the wilderness, he was allowed to remain with the Corps as a laborer until the following spring. Although he was repentant and worked extremely hard in the hope of having himself reinstated, the captains would not relent.

On August 20, near present-day Sioux City, the Corps of Discovery lost another man when Sergeant Charles Floyd died, apparently of a ruptured appendix. His comrades buried him on a bluff and commemorated him by naming a nearby river in his honor. Floyd's death could not have been averted under the best medical care of the day, which basically would have prescribed the same treatment given him by the captains—bleeding with lancets and purging with strong laxatives. Patrick Gass was elected sergeant in his place.

As the expedition moved on into present-day South Dakota, the men became increasingly concerned about the whereabouts of George Shannon, who had disappeared several days earlier while out hunting with Drouillard. With Shannon, who was carrying only a little ammunition, were the expedition's only two horses. After inadvertently becoming separated from Drouillard and the two horses, which had strayed, Shannon had rounded up the animals and sped on ahead to where he believed the boats would be. The only problem was that he had miscalculated the expedition's rate of progress, and the boats were behind him, not up ahead. Unknowing, frantic to catch up, Shannon continued to race on ahead. It was not until September 11 that the main body of the expedition overtook the young man, who was now weak from hunger after being out more than two weeks. A relieved Clark reflected, "thus a man had like to have Starved to death in a land of Plenty for the want of Bulletes or Something to kill his meat."

In terms of its wildlife, the territory the Corps passed through on this portion of its journey was literally a land of plenty. Among the "new" species that captains reported on in their journals were prairie dogs (called by Lewis "barking squirrels"), coyotes, pronghorn antelopes (Clark commented on the "agility and superior fleetness of this anamal," which he found "really astonishing"), jackrabbits, mule deers, and badgers. Clark was particularly fascinated by the badger, which he described as follows:

> his Shape & Size is like that of a Beaver, his head mouth &c. is like a Dogs with Short Ears, his Tail and Hair like that of a Ground Hog, and longer; and lighter. his Interals like the interals of a *Hog*, his Skin, thick and loose, his *Belly* is white and the Hair short, a white streek from his nose to his Shoulders.

The countryside the expedition now moved into was equally new and wondrous to the explorers. Beyond the stands of trees that continued to line the Missouri's shores, treeless terraces, broken by rugged, steep hills and dry gullies, stretched off into the distance. On the flat plains beyond the hills, buffalo grazed in huge numbers (at one point, Clark reported seeing 3,000 of the shaggy beasts in a herd), and the cries of magpies and hawks filled the air. Unlike later explorers in the region, such as Zebulon Pike, who described the region as the "great American desert," Lewis and Clark were favorably impressed by the High Plains. "Well-watered and beautiful" continued to be their most common description, and Lewis reserved his most negative commentary for the desolate regions between the Bitterroot Mountains and the Cascades. "What a field for a Botents [botanist] and a natirless [naturalist]," Clark exclaimed in his journal. At another point, he wrote:

> The Plains of this countrey are covered with a Leek Green Grass, well calculated for the sweetest and most norushing hay—interspersed with Cops [copses] of trees, Spreding ther lofty branchs over Pools Springs or Brooks of fine water. Groops of Shrubs covered with the most delicious froot is to be seen in every direction, and nature appears to have exerted herself to butify the Senery by the variety of

Earlier French travelers on the Missouri called the graceful pronghorn antelope cabril, or goat. Lewis reported disappointedly that "as they are watchfull and extreemly quick of sight and their sense of smelling very accute it is almost impossible to approach them within gunshot; in short they will frequently discover and flee from you at the distance of three miles."

The victory dance of the Teton Sioux, as painted by George Catlin. Clark wrote that in the course of the evening he and Lewis spent in a Teton Sioux village, "the Women Came forward highly Deckerated in their Way, with the Scalps and Trophies of War of their fathers Husbands Brothers or near Connections & proceeded to Dance the War Dance which they done with great Chearfullness until about 12 oClock."

flours Delicately and highly flavered raised above the Grass, which Strikes & profumes the Sensation, and amuses the mind throws it into Conjectering the cause of So magnificent a Senerey in a Country thus situated far removed from the Sivilised world to be enjoyed by nothing but the Buffalo Elk Deer & Bear in which it abounds & Savage Indians.

In late September, the Corps reached the vicinity of present-day Pierre, South Dakota, at the confluence of the Bad River and the Missouri, where it encountered a band of the Teton Sioux, or Dakota, Indians. An earlier council with the Yankton Sioux, downstream at the junction of the Missouri and the James River, had gone reasonably

well, although a Yankton chief, Half Man, had warned the explorers that "those nations above [upriver] will not open their ears."

The Teton Sioux were an impressive-looking people, clad in colorfully painted buffalo robes, their moccasins adorned with porcupine quills, hawk and eagle feathers in the hair of the warriors. They met the representatives of the U.S. government, who were clad in their finest dress uniforms, white ammunition belts crisscrossing the blue uniform shirts, under an American flag and an awning of sailcloth erected by Lewis on an island in the mouth of the Bad River.

As the Yankton Sioux had predicted, the meeting went badly. The Teton were regularly supplied with arms by their British trade connections farther north, and as the most powerful and feared Indian tribe in the region, they were used to charging tolls of Missouri River traders. They listened impassively to Lewis's standard speech promising friendship and commerce, translated imperfectly into sign language by Cruzatte and Labiche, and were unimpressed by the firing of the air gun and the demonstration of other technology. After some desultory conversation and exchange of gifts, including whiskey, the Indians became surly, demanded more presents, and would not allow Clark to return to the keelboat. The whites would not be allowed to proceed up the river unless they were willing to surrender one of the pirogues and all its goods, the Sioux explained. With this, the whites readied their weapons and made plain their intention to fight, and the Sioux backed off.

An uneasy truce prevailed. Heeding Jefferson's instructions to be "friendly and conciliatory" toward the Indians, Lewis and Clark even spent most of 2 evenings in the Sioux village, a collection of 80 buffalo-skin tipis surrounding a central lodge. There, the explorers feasted on roast dog, watched Indian dances conducted to the accompaniment of thumping drums and jingled antelope

Indians cross the Missouri River. By the time Lewis and Clark made contact with them, many of the tribes along the Missouri— in particular the Arikara, the Mandan, and the Hidatsa—had been greatly reduced in number as a result of disease. A smallpox epidemic in 1780–81, for example, had diminished the population of the Arikara by an estimated 75 percent.

hooves, and listened to the Sioux try to convince them why it was necessary that they monopolize the Missouri River trade. Yet the tensions of the initial encounter were never completely dispelled, and the whites remained fearful that the Sioux were planning a surprise attack; according to Clark, a Sioux prisoner of war, a member of the Omaha tribe, even confided as much to one of the Frenchmen. Lewis later called the Tetons "the vilest miscreants of the savage race" and the "pirates of the Missouri."

A few days later, on October 8, the Corps reached the earth lodge villages of the Arikara in northern South Dakota. They received a hospitable reception from this agricultural people, and the party remained with them for several days. The Arikara were essentially sedentary, as compared to the more nomadic Sioux, and they were somewhat intimidated by the troublesome Teton, who in Clark's words "poison their minds and keep them in perpetial [perpetual] dread," to the extent that the captains referred to them as the "slaves" of the Sioux. In the hope of forming an alliance against the Sioux, Lewis and Clark offered to make peace between the Arikara and their sometime enemies, the Mandan and Hidatsa. The Arikara welcomed this offer, and the usual presents and pleasantries were exchanged. The Indians were particularly awestruck by York, Clark's black servant, but as in the Sioux villages, Lewis and Clark were nonplussed by the Indian custom, intended as a gesture of hospitality, of making young women available for sexual favors.

Summer was rapidly drawing to an end, and there was no time to be wasted if the Corps was to reach the villages of the Mandan and Hidatsa by the coming of winter. Already, the days were growing short. The trees began to drop their leaves, and plants and shrubs started to fade. The men watched as migrating waterfowl passed overhead on their southward flights. At night, temperatures dipped to the freezing point, and in the morning there was frost on the buffalo grass. As October dwindled, the Corps pushed on toward its winter encampment—the most distant outpost of the new republic.

"This senery already rich pleasing and beautiful was still farther heightened by immence herds of Buffaloe, deer Elk and Antelopes which we saw in every direction feeding on the hills and plains," Lewis wrote on September 17. The Corps continued to encounter an unimaginable profusion of wildlife all the way up the Missouri River to its winter quarters at the Mandan villages.

Winter in the Wilderness

This morning early we fixed on the site for our
fortification which we immediately set about. This place
we have named Fort Mandan in honour of our
Neighbours.
> —Meriwether Lewis, November 2, 1805

These [Mandan] are the most friendly, well disposed
Indians inhabiting the missouri. They are brave, humane,
and hospitable.
> —William Clark, "Estimate of Eastern Indians"

In late October, as the Corps of Discovery made its way
up the Missouri River, it passed abandoned villages for-
merly inhabited by the Mandan Indians. These deserted
settlements attested to the tribe's weakened state—the
Mandan had been ravaged by a deadly smallpox epidemic
in the early 1780s—and to the ferocity of their traditional
enemies, the Sioux. On October 25, when the explorers
arrived at the outskirts of the lower Mandan village, they
were ogled by curious Indians who lined the banks and
called for them to come ashore. The Corps was now 164
days into its transcontinental journey and by its own estimate 1,600 miles away from Camp Dubois. Several days
later, under the customary awning and American flag,
Lewis and Clark conducted a successful council with their
soon-to-be neighbors for the winter.

*A Hidatsa warrior, as drawn by
the Swiss artist Karl Bodmer,
who visited the tribe in 1833.
Catlin described the Hidatsa as
taller and more heavily built
than their neighbors the
Mandan; the French called them
the Gros Ventres, or Big Bellies.
Lewis and Clark and most
subsequent visitors confirmed that
the Hidatsa were much more
warlike than the Mandan.*

A Mandan village, by Catlin. The Mandan and the Hidatsa lived in circular earth-covered lodges, 40 to 60 feet in diameter. The captains reported that at night the Indians brought their dogs and horses inside with them. When Catlin visited the Hidatsa in 1832, their elderly chief, Black Moccasin, asked the painter to extend his regards to Red Hair and Long Knife, his names for Lewis and Clark, whom he had met almost 30 years earlier.

The Mandan and their immediate neighbors to the north, the Hidatsa, lived in circular earth lodges in five separate villages near the mouth of the Knife River. The captains estimated their population at about 4,000 persons—the largest concentration of Indians on the Missouri River. The Mandan resided in the two lower villages, Mitutanka and Ruptáre, along the Missouri; the Hidatsa (called the Minitaris by Lewis and Clark) in the three upper settlements, Mahawha, Metaharta, and Menetarra, along the Knife. The Mandan and the Hidatsa were separate peoples, related culturally and linguistically, who had banded together for mutual protection against the Sioux.

Both were primarily agricultural peoples who grew corn, beans, and squash and gathered native plants to supplement their crops. Several times a year, both engaged in buffalo hunts on the nearby plains. The Hidatsa were the more aggressive of the two and ventured as far west as the Rocky Mountains to raid other tribes. Their travels made them excellent sources of geographical information for the captains. The Mandan were more inclined to stay close to home, and they fought only to fend off attacks by the Sioux and the Arikara.

The party began construction of their permanent winter headquarters, to be known as Fort Mandan, on November 3 and finished several weeks later. The fort was located on the east side of the Missouri, about 50 miles northwest of present-day Bismarck, North Dakota, a few miles below the mouth of the Knife River, nearly opposite the lower Mandan village. Sergeant Gass, a carpenter who probably supervised much of the construction work, described the structure as roughly triangular, with a row of huts along each of the 56-foot-long sides. The roofs of the huts sloped down from the outer side walls, which were about 18 feet high, and descended toward the center. The picketed front of the triangle, which faced the river, served as the fort's main gate, while a small enclosure filled a semicircular point at the rear. That shed was used to house the expedition's supplies, and its flat roof served as the sentry's watchtower. A trader for one of the British firms declared the fort "so strong as to be almost cannonball proof." This fortress would be the Corps' home for the next five months, during a bitter northern plains winter in which temperatures sometimes dropped to lower than 40 degrees below zero.

Clark described the party as maintaining good spirits for most of this time. Christmas and New Year's Day were celebrated with music, dancing, and alcoholic libations. Indians visited the fort frequently, and the chiefs, at least,

Bodmer's depiction of the buffalo dance of the Mandan, which the Indians themselves called the red stick ceremony. Part of the four-day ritual involved the acquisition of wisdom by young women (and ultimately their husbands) through sexual relations with the village elders. Clark regarded it as a "curious Custom."

expected to be entertained by the captains. In spite of the fierce cold, the men of the Corps were seldom idle. Hunting was necessary to provide meat—on an average day, the Corps consumed an entire buffalo, four deer, or a deer and an elk. To supplement its diet, the Corps traded war axes and other metal implements made by John Shields, the blacksmith, for crops from the village. Frequent socializing between the whites and the Indians became the norm, and liaisons between the men of the Corps and Indian women were commonplace. The captains did their best to treat an unfortunate consequence of these assignations—the transmission of venereal diseases. York was a particular favorite in the Indian villages, where a black man had never been seen before. The Hidatsa chief Le Borgne was so amazed by York's dark skin that he rubbed it with his moistened finger trying to remove the "paint."

The Hidatsa chief Le Borgne examines the skin of York, Clark's black slave. The tribes that the Corps encountered had never before seen a black man and often "flocked around him & examind him from top to toe," wrote Clark. Occasionally, York "carried on the joke and made himself more turribal than we wished him to doe."

Lewis and Clark were not the first white visitors to the Mandan-Hidatsa villages. Explorers and traders had arrived at the Knife River as early as 1738, and regular trade had been taking place since the 1790s. In fact, Indians of the High Plains had become accustomed to European manufactured goods, obtained through an intertribal trade network, even before the arrival of whites in their territory. European-produced goods simply became a new and much-desired component in a very active economic system. Among the Mandan and Hidatsa this indirect trade for European goods had been taking place for more than a century by the time Lewis and Clark arrived.

The Knife River villages in time became the central marketplace on the northern plains—a grand entrepôt of the Missouri trade system. The Mandan and Hidatsa were brokers in an international trade network that disbursed goods over thousands of miles: to the west and southwest with the Cheyenne, Crow, Kiowa, and Arapaho for horses and mules from the Spanish; to the north and northeast with the Cree and Assiniboine for European manufactured goods coming in from Hudson Bay; and to the east and southeast with the Sioux for eastern Indian items and additional European manufactures.

As middlemen in this intertribal network, the Mandan and Hidatsa warehoused horses and guns for distribution to tribes throughout the plains—often marking up prices 100 percent. This intertribal trade continued side by side with the European trade that began to develop in the 1790s once merchants from the Hudson's Bay and North West Fur companies of Canada came to bargain directly with the Mandan and Hidatsa, which enabled the Indians to increase their store of manufactured goods and solidify their position as the prime traders on the northern plains.

Lewis and Clark arrived among the Mandan and Hidatsa with two principal goals based on Jefferson's precepts. One was diplomatic—to apprise the tribes of the new sovereignty of the United States under the Louisiana Purchase

Indians hunt buffalo. Lewis and Clark's men engaged in several buffalo hunts with the Mandan and were impressed with the "great dexterity" of the Indians in killing the shaggy ruminants from horseback with arrows.

and to explain the purposes of their own mission. In this regard they also hoped to shift trade toward American interests at St. Louis and away from the English firms in Canada. They also wanted to establish intertribal peace; for the Mandan and Hidatsa that meant better relations with the Sioux and Arikara.

The Indians were not much interested in exploration, nor were they greatly concerned with the whites' notion of diplomacy, except as it immediately affected their commerce. Lewis and Clark were talking about trade over the long term, but the Mandan and Hidatsa, like the Sioux and Arikara before them, were more interested in the immediate exchange of goods. Lewis and Clark wanted to expand the commercial influence of the United States to enable it to compete with Great Britain; the Mandan and the Hidatsa wanted the best goods at the lowest price from the most dependable supplier and were not particularly worried about whether that supplier was British or American. Nor were the Indians prepared to make peace with their traditional enemies without some assurance of security, and they fully realized that the United States, despite the promises of Lewis and Clark, was not yet strong enough in the region to give them the meaningful assurances that they required. What would happen after the Corps of Discovery moved on? The United States had no trading posts in the area or soldiers to keep the peace.

The captains fared better in the other aspect of their mission to the Mandan and Hidatsa—the gathering of information in order to increase knowledge about the Indians' way of life. The men of the Corps obtained their information in a number of ways: by interviewing natives and traders who lived among them, by collecting cultural objects, by reporting on firsthand observations, and by participating in some Indian activities. The captains did their best work in recounting objective matters: describing villages, weapons, food, clothing, and other external aspects. They were not as good at subjective judgments or at describing ritualistic behavior, and they misunderstood and misinterpreted some activities they observed or participated in. They also missed some important ceremonies and activities because they stayed with the Indians for only a portion of the year.

Nonetheless, during their stay at Fort Mandan the captains did some of their best ethnographic work of the entire trip. In some ways, Lewis and Clark overcame their ethnocentric biases and were able to reach a genuine understanding of certain aspects of Indian culture. For example, they understood the status of chiefs among the Plains Indians and were able to recognize that the leaders' power arose from the consensus of their people. As Clark wrote: "Power is merely the acquiescence of the warriors in the superior merit of a chief."

Soon after arriving at the Indian villages, the captains hired René Jusseaume (sometimes spelled Jessaume), an independent trader who had lived with the Mandan for about 15 years, as an interpreter. Another French trader, Jean Baptiste Lepage, was made a member of the permanent party to replace John Newman, who was discharged for an act of insubordination back at the Arikara village. Lepage had previously ventured some distance up the Missouri, and Clark wished to make use of his knowledge in preparing the map of the West he was working on at Fort Mandan.

Another new addition was the French Canadian trader, Toussaint Charbonneau, who was signed on because of his knowledge of Hidatsa. He had lived among the tribe for several years. Joining him as a member of the party was one of his two Shoshone wives, Sacagawea, who had been captured by a Hidatsa war party in 1800, when she was about 13 years old. It was hoped that Sacagawea would serve as an intermediary and interpreter when the Corps met the Shoshone in the Rocky Mountains. That winter, on February 11, 1805, she gave birth to a baby boy, Jean Baptiste. This infant, whom Clark referred to by the affectionate nickname Pomp, accompanied the expedition, on his mother's back, all the way to the Pacific; the presence of the Indian woman and her child would help dispel Indian fears that the Corps of Discovery was a war party. Although Sacagawea certainly played an instrumental role in the success of the expedition, she was in no way its primary guide, as she has sometimes been portrayed.

As spring approached and the ice in the Missouri broke up, the captains prepared to resume their westward journey. They also readied the return party for its departure. Corporal Warfington and a small squad of soldiers, the remaining French boatmen, and the two expelled men, Reed and Newman, were to take the keelboat back to St. Louis. With them, intended for Jefferson's eyes, went the captains' journals completed to that date, tables of observations, letters, maps, and a large number of natural history specimens. This latter category included samples of the plants, shrubs, grasses, and trees of the Great Plains—

among them buffalo berry, Indian tobacco, sagebrush, big bluestem, and cottonwood—as well as animal skins and several live animals, including four magpies and a prairie dog. Selected artifacts of the Plains Indians were also boxed up for Jefferson's inspection. Also included was an "Estimate of Eastern Indians" (those east of the Rocky Mountains), the captains' comments on the Indian tribes they had encountered, and Clark's partly conjectural map of the West, which was based on his own travels and information given him by fur traders and Indians. The map was extremely detailed and accurate regarding the lands the Corps of Discovery had traveled through, based as it was on a series of 29 maps Clark had drawn along the way, necessarily less so concerning the regions still to come. As a supplement to the map the captains included a narrative summary of rivers, creeks, and "remarkable places" along the Missouri.

Five weeks short of a year after leaving Camp Dubois, the party was set to go. Half a continent remained ahead of the Corps before it would reach the Pacific. On April 3, four days before the actual departure, an eager and impatient Clark wrote, "we Shall . . . Set out tomorrow."

The interior of a Mandan lodge, by Bodmer. A framework of poles and timber supported the earthen exterior of the lodge, which was often home to as many as 40 people. Mandan lodges were built close together, with just room enough for a pedestrian or rider to pass between them. In good weather, the Mandan were fond of sitting out on their roofs.

To the Rockies

We were now about to penetrate a country at least two thousand miles in width, on which the foot of civillized man had never trodden. . . . Entertain[in]g as I do, the most confident hope of succeading in a voyage which had formed a da[r]ling project of mine for the last ten years, I could but esteem this moment of my departure as among the most happy of my life.

—Meriwether Lewis, April 7, 1805

A bracing 28 degrees greeted the explorers on the morning of April 7, 1805, but by the time of departure the temperature had climbed to a balmy 64 and a brisk wind pushed against the pirogues. Bidding farewell to the St. Louis–bound keelboat and its occupants, the permanent party set out at 4:00 P.M. The Corps of Discovery now numbered 33 persons: the 2 captains, 3 sergeants (Ordway, Pryor, and Gass), 2 interpreters (Drouillard and Charbonneau), 23 privates, York, Sacagawea, and the infant Jean Baptiste. The end of the season at Fort Mandan marked an important transition. Difficult and potentially dangerous as the route had been thus far, others had ventured over it before them and had already mapped the way. From Fort Mandan on the Corps entered country about which they had only speculative information.

Lewis was in a buoyant mood that afternoon and took to shore to walk to that night's encampment, probably accompanied by faithful Seaman. That night Lewis returned to his diary after a long period of infrequent writing; he would keep a steady record until August, when the

Bodmer's portrait of an Assiniboin warrior. The Assiniboin were one tribe the captains did not wish to encounter; on May 10, 1805, Lewis wrote, "We still beleive ourselves in the country usually hunted by the Assinniboins, and as they are a vicious ill disposed nation we think it best to be on our guard."

frequency of his entries fell off once again. His first entry reflects the elation he felt at the Corps' being on the move once again:

> Our vessels consisted of six small canoes, and two large perogues. This little fleet altho' not quite so rispectable as those of Columbus or Capt. Cook were still viewed by us with as much pleasure as those deservedly famed adventurers ever beheld theirs; and I dare say with quite as much anxiety for their safety and preservation. . . . The party are in excellent health and sperits, zealously attatched to the enterprise, and anxious to proceed; not a whisper or murmur of discontent to be heard among them, but all act in unison, and with the most perfect harmony.

As the explorers moved west along the Missouri into the present-day state of Montana, the terrain grew more arid and rugged. There were far fewer trees, and the grassy prairies of the Great Plains gave way to a region of sage-brush, juniper, and drought-tolerant short grasses. Still, Lewis sighted cottonwood, willow, elm, ash, and box elder trees along the river's banks, and the underbrush contained rose bushes, honeysuckle, currants, serviceberries, and chokecherries.

The captains also recorded their observations of new animals, such as the bighorn sheep, and the famed grizzly bear made its appearance. The hunters had discounted the many stories they had heard about the ferocity of *Ursus horribilis*, as the grizzly is known in Latin nomenclature, and they professed to be anxious to meet one. A first and limited encounter occurred on April 29, near the Yellow-stone River, when Lewis and a companion wounded two grizzlies. One bear pursued the captain but was so badly hurt that Lewis was able to reload and kill him. The con-fident captain wrote: "the Indians may well fear this an-amal . . . but in the hands of a skillfull riflemen they are by no means as formidable or dangerous as they have been represented." He would soon feel less assured.

A bear killed on May 5 near the Milk River proved more formidable. Lewis wrote: "It was . . . extreemly hard to kill notwithstanding he had five balls through his lungs and five others in various parts he swam more than half the distance acoss the river to a sandbar & it was at least twenty minutes before he died." After the Corps spotted a grizzly on the following day, Lewis commented in his journal that "the curiossity of our party is pretty well satisfyed with rispect to this anamal . . . [the grizzly] has staggered the resolution of several of them, others however seem keen for action with the bear." About a week later, William Bratton, who was walking along the shore, shot a bear. His companions on the water were startled when Bratton came charging out of the forest, screaming in terror; the enraged grizzly had chased him for half a mile. A party of seven, including Lewis, went ashore and tracked

A grizzly bear attempts to escape its pursuers. In noting the ways in which grizzlies differed from the black bear with which he and his fellow easterners were familiar, Lewis wrote that the grizzly was a "much more furious and formidable animal." He also noted that when the Indians were about to embark on a grizzly hunt, they prepared for it as if "they are about to make war uppon a neighboring nation."

the wounded beast to its lair, where several shots were
necessary to kill it. In his journal, Lewis confessed to now
being "intimidated" by the magnificent predator; "I must
confess that I do not like the gentlemen and had reather
fight two Indians than one bear," he wrote. This new

Alfred Jacob Miller's Buffaloes Drinking and Bathing at Night. *Lewis wrote of the Missouri, "This immense river so far as we have yet ascended, waters one of the fairest portions of the globe, nor do I believe that there is in the universe a similar extent of country."*

respect informed Lewis's future behavior. For example, in his journal entry for May 12, he wrote:

> I walked on shore this morning for the benefit of exersize which I much wanted, and also to exmaine the country and its productions, in these excurtions I most generally

went alone armed with my rifle . . . thus equiped I feel myself more than an equal match for a brown bear provided I get him in open woods or near the water, but feel myself a little diffident with respect to an attack in the open plains. I have therefore come to a resolution to act on the defencive only, should I meet these gentlemen in the open plains.

Those eager for another encounter got their chance on May 14, not far from the Musselshell River, when a shore party of six hunters went after a single grizzly. A volley of four balls ripped into the animal, but it simply charged ahead, took two more rounds from a second volley, and kept coming. One of the balls broke the animal's shoulder, slowing it slightly, but even so it was on the hunters faster than they could believe. The terrified men fled pell-mell toward the river. Two made it to a canoe while the others took cover, hastily reloaded, and fired again. When the bear turned on the shooters, they flung aside their rifles and plunged 20 feet off an embankment, the grizzly tumbling after them into the water. Finally a rifleman on shore put a round through the bear's brain, killing it instantly. Eight balls were found in its carcass.

Lewis had his own encounter a month later at the Missouri's Great Falls when, while out hunting alone, he noticed a large grizzly approaching. As he raised his gun to shoot, he realized he had not reloaded after earlier killing a buffalo. With the bear at his heels he took off across the plains, plunged into the river, and turned to face the bear with his espontoon (an officer's lance), but to his surprise and relief the bear lumbered away.

But these adventures were merely interludes amid the day-to-day work. The Corps made good progress, and in his journal Lewis exulted in the beauty and richness of the country. Beaver lodges were seen frequently along the river, and

the whol face of the country was covered with herds of Buffaloe, Elk & Antelopes; deer are also abundant, but keep themselves more concealed in the woodland. The buffaloe Elk and Antelope are so gentle that we pass near them while feeding, without apearing to excite any alarm among them; and when we attract their attention, they frequently approach us more nearly to discover what we are, and in some instances pursue us a considerable distance apparenly with that view.

Needless to say, the hunting was very good and the Corps ate well; but the weather was not as favorable. Ice still coated the river on some mornings, it occasionally snowed, and the men were frequently lashed by clouds of sand whipped off the riverbanks and sandbars by the constant wind. The blowing sand irritated the eyes and skin and got into clothes and gear, making all very uncomfortable.

Audubon's painting of the gray wolf of North America. Clark reported gray wolves to be "verry numourous"; Lewis wrote that "we scarcely see a gang of buffaloe without observing a parsel of these faithfull shepherds on their skirts in readiness to take care of the mamed wounded."

From the high cliffs that line the upper Missouri, Indians look down at the Corps of Discovery as it makes its way upriver. The Corps often detected signs of the presence of Indians without actually making contact; in several cases, such as when the Indians in question were likely Assiniboin or Blackfeet, the captains were happy to avoid an encounter.

On April 25, Lewis led a small patrol ahead of the main party in order to reach the Yellowstone River and take astronomical readings. For the explorers this spot effectively divided the known world from the unknown; as far as they knew no one but Indians had ventured beyond this point. They would not reenter lands known to the outside world again until they neared the Pacific Ocean. Clark and the main party arrived the next day, and to celebrate the occasion rations of whiskey were passed round, Cruzatte broke out his fiddle, and the men danced and sang well into the evening. Two days were spent at this site, resting and allowing soaked gear to dry out; then the party moved on, into the future state of Montana.

On May 14, the same day the party of six hunters had their terrifying encounter with the grizzly, Lewis and Clark were also both ashore—an unusual circumstance. Charbonneau temporarily had control of the main pirogue, which contained the party's most important articles, including papers, instruments, medicine, and a large share of the Indian trade goods. Suddenly a squall of wind struck, ripping the pirogue's sail from the hands of a boatman and the tiller from Charbonneau and flinging the boat on its side. Charbonneau, whom Lewis called the "most timid waterman in the world," was too frightened (he could not swim) to do anything to right the craft, but Cruzatte, an expert boatman, proved equal to the situation. After threatening to shoot Charbonneau if he did not reclaim the rudder, Cruzatte ordered several men to bail water and row toward the shore, where the boat arrived barely above water. All the while Sacagawea, with tiny Jean Baptiste in one hand, calmly bailed water or collected floating items with the other. Lewis, who had been watching helplessly from shore, was nearly beside himself with anger and frustration. The loss of the pirogue's contents, among which were some of the journals, would have been devastating. It had been quite a day for the Corps of Discovery; that night, as Lewis wrote:

> After having all matters arranged for the evening as well as the nature of circumstances would permit, we thought it a proper occasion to console ourselves and cheer the sperits of our men and accordingly took a drink of grog and gave each man a gill of sperits.

All along, the captains had been supplying names to undesignated rivers, creeks, and physical features. As the explorers proceeded through new country, such opportunities increased, and landmarks soon honored virtually every member of the party. In late May, the expedition reached a large stream that entered the Missouri from the south; Clark named it the Judith, after Julia (or Judith)

Hancock, a girl in the States whom he later married. Lewis later imitated Clark by naming the Marias River after a cousin, Maria Wood. Less provoking of romantic reveries was the discovery, near the Judith, of dozens of rotting buffalo carcasses at the foot of an impressive precipice, over which, Lewis reported, the Indians of the region would drive a herd as part of their seasonal hunts. A "great many wolves" prowled among the remains; Lewis reported that the easy pickings had made the wolves "fat and ex- treemly gentle."

The expedition had entered a region known as the Breaks of the Missouri, also called the Mauvaises Terres, or Badlands, by later French travelers. It is a land of bro- ken, dark terrain and impressive geological formations. On the western end of the Breaks lie the spectacular White Cliffs. Lewis's journal passages celebrate the harsh beauty of this rugged territory. He was especially struck by white sandstone outcroppings embedded in black igneous rocks, while erosion created fanciful forms in his mind and en- livened his prose:

> With the immagination and an oblique view at a distance,
> [the rocks] are made to represent eligant ranges of lofty
> freestone buildings. . . . As we passed on it seemed as if
> those seens of visionary inchantment would never have
> and end . . . so perfect indeed are those walls that I
> should have thought that nature had attempted here to
> rival the human art of masonry had I not recollected that
> she had first began her work.

The landscape was as rugged as it was wondrous, however, and the river grew shallower and swifter. Rapids made the fleet's progress difficult, and the strength of the current and opposing winds made it necessary once more for the men to resort to the towrope. As the men labored along the river's edge (and sometimes in the icy water itself), where sharp stones cut right through their moccasins, Rocky Mountain sheep capered gracefully above them on the rugged hillsides. Lewis devoted several paragraphs in

(continued on page 81)

The Fairest Portion

A Mandan couple, by Karl Bodmer.

It might be said that America's infatuation with the Far West—that magnificent region of wide-open spaces, endless, rolling prairies, untamed rivers, lonesome canyons, and towering mountains stretched out beneath a limitless sky; the silence of its expanses broken by the screech of an eagle, the rumble of a stampeding buffalo herd miles wide, the thunder of foaming rapids, or the howling of coyotes under a rising moon; inhabited by an astonishing profusion of wildlife and a host of proud Indian nations—began with the voyage of Lewis and Clark up the Missouri and on to the Pacific. Certainly, the captains provided the United States with its first inkling of the full extent and splendor of the western lands. The painters whose works illustrate the pages of this section did not visit the West until several decades after Lewis and Clark, but their creations nonetheless give visual form to the peoples and places the captains described so evocatively in their journals.

Bodmer's portrait of a Piegan Blackfoot chief, Mehkskehme-Sukahs, or Iron Shirt. The Swiss painter visited the West with his noble patron, Prince Maximilian of Wied Neuwied, in 1833. On their way west, they stopped at St. Louis, where they struck up a friendship with Clark, who was then serving as territorial governor.

Old Bear, a Mandan medicine man, by George Catlin, whose
artistic ambition was the "production of a literal and graphic
delineation of the living manners, customs, and character of an
interesting race of people who are rapidly passing away from the
face of the earth—lending a hand to a dying nation, who have no
historians or biographers of their own to portray with fidelity their
native looks and history."

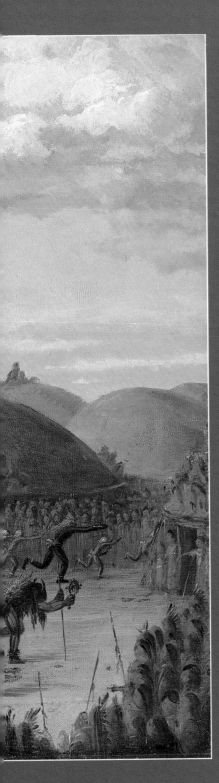

Catlin's portrayal of the O-kee-pa ceremony, or
bull dance, of the Mandan. Catlin's account of
the ceremony, which culminated in young
Mandan warriors being hung from the roof of the
medicine lodge by bone and wooden skewers
thrust through their pectoral and back muscles,
was initially disbelieved. Lewis and Clark
apparently did not witness this ceremony during
their time with the Mandan.

John Mix Stanley's Scene on the Columbia River. *Stanley, a native of Canandaigua, New York, was inspired to go west by Catlin's gallery of Indian pictures. On the first leg of their voyage, the captains were less susceptible to the scenic beauty of the Pacific Northwest than Stanley, although Clark later had great praise for the Willamette Valley.*

Bodmer's View of the Stone Walls of the upper Missouri, which Lewis said "exhibit a most romantic appearance." The romanticism with which Bodmer, Catlin, and Stanley imbued their vision of the West owed in large part to their realization that it was on the verge of being changed forever by American settlement, a process that began with the expedition of Lewis and Clark and the Corps of Discovery.

(continued from page 72)
his journal to a description of this elegant animal, which was previously unknown to all but the Indians.

On May 26, Lewis climbed to the top of a hill and for the first time glimpsed what he thought were the snow-capped Rockies. Although what Lewis saw was actually the Bears Paw Mountains, not the Rockies, which were still 100 miles farther west, he was still able to anticipate with elation the Corps' imminent completion of one of their main ojectives—the reaching of the headwaters of the Missouri.

On May 26, 1805, Lewis wrote that after ascending a high bluff "I beheld the Rocky Mountains for the first time." But, he added, "when I reflected on the difficulties which this snowey barrier would most probably throw in my way to the Pacific . . . it in some measure counterballanced the joy I had felt in the first few minutes I gazed at them."

In early June the Corps arrived at the confluence of the Missouri and the Marias, as Lewis named the more northerly of the two streams. Because the Hidatsa had not told them of its existence, the Marias presented something of a dilemma to the explorers. The captains had to determine which stream was the true Missouri, knowing that a wrong decision might cost them valuable time and strand them in the Rockies during the winter. Initial reconnaissances correctly convinced them that the river to the southwest was the Missouri, although most of the party believed otherwise. After nearly a week the captains' belief was confirmed when Lewis and an advance party discovered the Great Falls of the Missouri, which the Indians had told them about.

Lewis called the Great Falls the "grandest sight I ever beheld." He wished that he

> might be enabled to give to the enlightened world some just idea of this truly magnifficent and sublimely grand object, which has from the commencement of time been concealed from the view of civilized man; but this was fruitless and vain. . . . I hope still to give to the world some faint idea of an object which at this moment fills me with such pleasure and astonishment, and which of it's kind I will venture to ascert is second to but one in the known world.

The falls were stunningly beautiful, but they presented a considerable obstacle, for the Corps would have to find a way to carry all their supplies, including the boats, around them. Clark's carefully conducted survey showed that a portage of about 18 miles would be necessary to skirt the falls. From cottonwood trees and the masts of the pirogues, the men of the Corps constructed wagon frames, on which they placed the supply-laden canoes. All excess items were buried for retrieval later. The white pirogue was carefully concealed in some underbrush; the same had been done to the red pirogue back at the Marias. The portage was backbreaking labor. There were no horses to pull the wagons; the men hauled these tremendous loads across rough ground infested with prickly pear cactus, whose needles jabbed through their elk-skin clothing and moccasins. Blazing heat alternated with chilling winds and storms so ferocious that hailstones left the men of the Corps bleeding; at one point, Clark, Sacagawea, and Charbonneau were almost swept away by a flash flood. The men grew so tired that at each of the frequent rest stops that Lewis ordered, many of them immediately sank into sleep. Lewis recorded that at other times some of them simply passed out from the heat and their exertion; "their fatiegues are incredible," he wrote. So many grizzlies prowled the area around their campsites that the captains forbade anyone from venturing into the brush alone. Yet despite the hardships, Lewis reported that "no one complains, all go with cheerfullness." On one trip along the portage route some ingenious fellows even hoisted a sail over one of the wagons in order to take advantage of the wind. "This is really sailing on dry land," Lewis commented.

All told, the portage took almost a month to complete. Lewis, despite his appreciation for the herculean labors performed by his men, endured the latter part of this span with some impatience. With scarce comprehension of the endeavors, obstacles, and miles yet ahead of him, he confided to his journal that he was reluctantly relinquishing hope of crossing the Rockies, reaching the Pacific, and returning to Fort Mandan by the onset of winter.

There was also a more immediate disappointment for him to confront. Beyond the falls, Lewis put together the iron-frame, collapsible boat he had designed at Harpers Ferry and carried across the continent. Unfortunately, the lack of pine trees at the falls made it impossible to obtain the tar necessary to waterproof its buffalo-skin exterior, and the craft, aptly dubbed the *Experiment*, simply would not float. The failure of his invention embarrassed Lewis, but the only solution was to construct two more dugout canoes and proceed on.

Upriver from the falls the party at last entered the Rockies, passing through the spectacular canyon the explorers called the Gates of the Mountains, near today's Helena, Montana. Beautiful canyon walls towering 1,200 feet above the river did not, however, relieve sore feet and aching muscles. The Corps was now anxiously seeking the Shoshone, from whom they hoped to purchase horses for the journey over the mountains. Sacagawea began to recognize familiar landmarks, and on July 25, Clark, leading an overland patrol, reached the point where the Missouri converges from three forks. The Indians had told the captains that the westernmost fork would take them to a short portage across the Continental Divide. Lewis arrived at the Three Forks with the remainder of the boat party two days later, only to find his friend Clark utterly exhausted and quite ill. For this reason, and so as to allow the other men to rest their blistered feet and sore backs and Lewis time to obtain accurate astronomical readings, the party remained at the Three Forks for several days.

Sacagawea informed the captains that they were encamped on the exact spot where her people had camped when she had been captured five years earlier. Lewis was surprised that she seemed to show no emotion, either at the recollection of that event or at the prospect of meeting her people. He wrote that he believed that "if she has enough to eat and a few trinkets to wear . . . she would be perfectly content anywhere."

The captains decided to name the three rivers the Jefferson, the Madison, and the Gallatin, after the president and his secretaries of state and treasury, James Madison and Albert Gallatin. The Corps set off on the Jefferson, the westernmost stream, on July 30. Leaving the ailing Clark behind with the boat party, Lewis pushed ahead overland with a few men—Shields, Hugh McNeal, and

Drouillard, who was perhaps the Corps' most reliable man in the wilderness—to try to make contact with the Shoshone. On August 12 this party finally came to the head of the small stream—a tributary of the Beaverhead, which he had followed from its juncture with the Jefferson—that Lewis regarded as the ultimate source of "the heretofore deemed endless Missouri," but his joy at drinking from those waters was tempered by his realization that the portage to the Columbia River would not be as easy as he had hoped. Lewis had expected that once across the Rockies, a short portage would take the Corps to the Columbia, which would flow across an easily traversed plain all the way to the ocean. Instead, atop a ridge at today's Lemhi Pass on the Montana-Idaho border, he saw further ranges of snowcapped mountains stretching out along the horizon.

The Shoshone ford a river. Lewis wrote of his initial encounter with three Shoshone chiefs: "These men then advanced and embraced me very affectionately in their way which is by putting their left arm over your wright sholder clasping your back, while they apply their left cheek to yours and frequently vociforate the word âh-hí-e, âh-hí-e that is I am much pleased, I am much rejoiced."

Fur traders meet with the
Shoshone, as painted by Miller,
a European-trained American
artist who was the first to paint
the mountain men from life.
More than 30 years earlier, Lewis
found that although the Shoshone
lived in a "wretched stait of
poverty . . . they are not only
cheerfull but even gay." He
admired their democratic spirit:
"Each individual is his own
sovereign master, and acts from
the dictates of his own mind . . .
every man is a chief."

The next day Lewis's party entered the valley of the Lemhi River and made its first contact with the Shoshone, a war party of 60 that took the whites back to their encampment. The Indians were initially very wary of the whites, and Lewis had a hard time persuading them to accompany him back through the Lemhi Pass and to the Jefferson, where he expected to rendezvous with Clark and the remainder of the Corps. He succeeded only by letting the Indians know, in sign language, that he considered them cowards for their refusal. This affront to their pride was enough to convince them to accompany him and his men.

The reunion on August 17 was a joyous one, for the Indians as well as the whites, because it turned out that the Shoshone chief, Cameahwait, was Sacagawea's brother. This kinship helped bring about good relations, and after a council and much diplomacy the Corps was able to purchase from the Indians the horses it required. The Shoshone also told them that the river routes through the mountains were impassable, but they did provide information about an overland trail to the north sometimes used by the Nez Percé Indians. During his time with the Shoshone, Lewis had time to record his impression of the tribe. Despite their richness in horses and their flair as horsemen, the Shoshone were a poor people who often had barely enough food to subsist on. At one time, their access to horses, obtained from southern tribes such as the Comanche, had enabled them to dominate the plains, but once the Blackfeet, the Hidatsa, and the Sioux began to obtain guns from British traders, the Shoshone were driven into the mountains. By Lewis and Clark's time they were a people of two traditions, digging camas roots and fishing for salmon in the mountains part of the year, then venturing out onto the plains to hunt buffalo when starvation forced them to. It was the captains' promise that future American visitors to the region would bring trade goods, including rifles, to the Shoshone that convinced them to cooperate with the Corps of Discovery. Lewis found them "frank, communicative, fair in dealing, generous with the little they possess, extreemly honest, and by no means beggarly."

On August 18, while at Camp Fortunate, the captains' name for the site along the forks of the Beaverhead River where they met with the Shoshone, Lewis celebrated his 31st birthday and penned a reflective passage. Disregarding his considerable achievements, he pledged to redouble his efforts at improving himself and in the future to "live for *mankind*, as I have heretofore lived *for myself*." In the days ahead, the struggle to cross the mountains would require redoubled efforts on the part of every member of the Corps of Discovery.

Mountains, Deserts, and Sea

we Suped [on] a little portable Soup. the most of the party is weak and feeble Suffering with hunger. our horses feet are gitting Sore and fall away in these mountains, but we are in hopes to git out of them Soon.
—Joseph Whitehouse, September 19, 1805

On August 24, Lewis wrote that he had "the inexpressible satisfaction to find myself once more under way." Yet ahead of him and the Corps loomed one of the most difficult periods of the entire trip. The party now faced its greatest physical challenge — crossing the rugged Bitterroot Range, as the portion of the Rocky Mountains along the present-day border of Montana and Idaho is now known.

Clark's reconnaissance of the nearby Salmon River confirmed what the Shoshone had told the captains—there was no easy river route to the Columbia. Although the river flowed toward the Columbia, it was unnavigable because of rapids. Moreover, sheer cliffs and precipices along its banks made land travel along it equally impractical; the perilous stream has since earned the nickname the "River of No Return." The scarcity of game and the unsuitability of the available timber for canoes were additional deterrents. After carefully weighing all the options, the captains decided to cross the mountains on horseback along a route to be shown them by a Shoshone guide, Old Toby.

On August 30, the explorers set out northward from the Shoshone encampment on the Lemhi River, on the west

On November 3, 1805, Clark recorded seeing Mount Hood in the distance, approximately 47 miles away. The captains were gladdened by sightings of such named landmarks, which meant they were leaving uncharted territory for regions previously visited by British and American ships.

side of the Lemhi Pass, while the Shoshone set out eastward toward the Three Forks for their seasonal buffalo hunt. The Corps followed the Lemhi, a negotiable portion of the Salmon, and then the North Fork of the Salmon through difficult terrain along a ridge of the Bitterroots near the Continental Divide. The Shoshone had sold the explorers about 30 horses; probably the captains, Sacagawea, and perhaps a few others rode, but most of the animals were used as beasts of burden, and the majority of the men walked, leading a heavily laden pack animal. "Horrid bad going," Whitehouse called it on one of the worst days. On September 3, Old Toby led them through a pass at the divide near present-day Lost Trail Pass and they crossed from modern Idaho back into Montana. The next day, at a spot later much favored by fur trappers, who called it Ross's Hole, they came upon a tribe of Salish Indians. (The Salish are often called the Flatheads, apparently from the sign-language designation for the tribe— hands pressed flat against either side of the skull.) Like the Shoshone, the Salish were rich in horses but somewhat short of food at the time and had been driven from the plains to the mountains by fiercer tribes. With Sacagawea and a Shoshone captive of the Salish serving as interpreters, the party was able to barter for additional mounts for their herd and increase it to more than 40 animals.

On September 4, 1805, Lewis and Clark met with a group of Flathead Indians at a spot later known as Ross's Hole. The term Flathead *was used for a number of different Indian tribes, few of whom actually practiced head deformation. Clark recorded the name of the Indians at Ross's Hole as the Tushepau; he said they numbered 400, lived in 33 lodges, and owned 500 horses.*

After two days with the Salish, the Corps headed north along the Bitterroot River, which Lewis first named the Flathead and later the Clark's. At the same time, the Indians set out for their rendezvous along the Missouri with the Shoshone. Aware that an even more difficult road lay ahead, the leaders decided to take advantage of clear skies and fair weather in order to rest and prepare themselves for the coming trek out of the mountains. On September 9, 1805, they established camp a few miles south of today's Missoula, Montana, on a little stream they christened Travelers Rest Creek. (It is now known as Lolo Creek.) There, they spent two days taking celestial observations, repacking and adjusting loads, hunting game (with mixed success), and resting up for the trip ahead. A passing Indian joined the party briefly and confirmed that a stream to the west, just five days' march ahead, was navigable all the way to the ocean.

In fact, it would take the Corps 11 harrowing days—perhaps the severest physical test of the entire expedition—to descend from the Bitterroots via the Lolo Trail. Winter was already beginning in the high country, and the party struggled through deepening snow along narrow, rocky mountain paths. Some of the horses lost their footing and fell to their deaths, carrying with them precious supplies and equipment, including Clark's field desk. Game was difficult to find, and the party was forced to stave off hunger by eating some of their packhorses. Old Toby misled them at one point, adding time and miles to their hardships. On September 16, one of the worst days, Clark wrote, "I have been wet and as cold in every part as I ever was in my life," and he feared that his thinly clad feet would freeze.

In spite of these hardships, the captains did not cease their scientific pursuits. In one five-day period, Lewis described common snowberry, western trumpet honeysuckle, and mountain huckleberry (all expedition discoveries); the varied thrush and the Pacific mountain ash, whose

Miller painted this picture of travelers in the West conferring with their Indian guide. Lewis and Clark relied heavily on geographic information provided them by the Indians. The Shoshone woman Sacagawea earned much fame for her assistance in directing the Corps, but the contributions of several Nez Percé guides were even more crucial.

red berries the bird favored; three new species of grouse—the blue, the spruce, and the Oregon ruffed grouse; Steller's jay, the gray jay, and Lewis's woodpecker (named later for the captain). Clark had earlier described a bird that would one day bear his name, Clark's nutcracker. Moreover, through the Bitterroots the captains recorded careful observations of Rocky Mountain trees (including some unknown to science), such as the grand, Douglas, and subalpine fir; whitebark, lodgepole, ponderosa, and western white pine; Sitka alder; western larch; Engelmann spruce; and western red cedar.

As the situation in the mountains approached desperation—many of the men were growing weak with hunger, and the last expendable horse had been slaughtered—the captains decided to send Clark ahead with a small detachment to find open country and make contact with Indians. Clark set out with six men on September 18 and arrived two days later at Weippe Prairie, an open area southeast of present-day Orofino, Idaho, where he found a Nez Percé encampment. The Indians were generous with what food they had—roots of the camas lily and dried salmon—and on the 21st Clark sent Reuben Field back with fish and roots and to guide the main party in. (Along with salmon, camas roots were the staple food of the Nez Percé. The roots were either eaten raw, steamed, or after

At Weippe Prairie, not far from the Clearwater River on the far side of the mountains, Clark found a Nez Percé encampment. The captains were greatly relieved to be out of the mountains, particularly once the Indians informed them they could reach the Columbia by water.

being pounded into flour and baked. Sergeant Gass thought they tasted like pumpkins.) Although it was now obvious that there was no easily navigable water route from the Mississippi to the Pacific, as Jefferson had so fervently hoped there would be, the captains were excited by the prospect of completing their mission. "The pleasure I now felt in having tryumphed over the rocky Mountains," Lewis wrote, "and decending once more to a level and fertile country where there was every rational hope of finding a comfortable subsistence for myself and party can be more readily conceived than expressed."

On September 23, the day after Lewis's arrival, the captains held their usual council, this time with Twisted Hair, the ranking chief of the Nez Percé while the other leaders were away with a war party. The customary medals and gifts were passed out, and inquiries were made about the route ahead. Nez Percé, or "pierced noses," is the name given these people by French traders who later visited them; Lewis and Clark called them the Chopunnish, a phonetic spelling of their name for themselves. In their journals, the captains commented on the tribe's hospitality, their nasal ornaments (from which the French appellation derived), and their fine Appaloosa horses. The Lolo Trail was their route across the mountains.

From the Indians, the captains learned that the Corps could now return to the water for their passage to the sea. From September 26 to October 7, the Corps and some Indians camped at a spot about five miles west of present-day Orofino, on the south side of the Clearwater River opposite the mouth of the North Fork Clearwater, called the Kooskooskee and Chopunnish rivers by the captains. At Canoe Camp, the explorers built dugout canoes for the downriver trip and recuperated from the mountain crossing.

By October 7, the Corps, supplemented by a couple of Nez Percé guides, was ready to move on again. The horses were left with the Nez Percé, to be reclaimed on the return journey. Traveling in five dugout canoes hewn from local trees, the Corps rushed swiftly—slowed occasionally by capsizings and portages around rapids—down the Clearwater and Snake rivers to the Great Columbian Plain, yet another ecosystem never before visited by white Americans. Beyond the walls of the river canyon, the land was parched, the vegetation scraggly. There were few trees and no game; only prickly pear cactus seemed able to thrive in this "barren and broken" land. The way of life of the native inhabitants, mostly Nez Percé and Yakima, also differed from those they had encountered before. These new tribes depended on canoes rather than horses for transportation, and they fished and gathered roots rather than hunted. Clark found them to be generally poorer than the Plains Indians, but of a "mild disposition," "stout and likely." Many of them suffered from blindness and poor teeth, which Clark attributed to the constant glare of sunlight off water and snow and their poor diet. Great numbers of these Indians lived along the riverbanks and sold the men of the Corps dried salmon and roots in exchange for trade goods. When they grew tired of this monotonous diet, some of the men bought dogs to eat. Lewis enjoyed dog meat; Clark never developed a taste for it.

On October 16, the Corps at last reached the Columbia. Strangely, this long-awaited moment elicited no written feelings of elation, satisfaction, or accomplishment from Clark, who was the only one of the captains making journal entries at this time. At the confluence of the Snake and Columbia, the Corps established camp and spent 2 days scouting the area, taking astronomical observations, meeting with Yakima and Wanapam Indians, and purchasing 40 dogs as a food source for the final push to the ocean. They also observed the end of the great seasonal salmon run on the Columbia. While Lewis compiled a vocabulary of the local Indian languages, Clark did a little hunting, killing several "prairie cocks" (sage grouse) and ducks, which were no doubt a welcome supplement to the men's diet.

Indians catch salmon at the Colville Falls on the Columbia River. Lewis and Clark never visited this portion of the Columbia, but they had ample opportunity to witness the methods of fishing used by the Indians living along the river.

The Indians had warned the captains that they would encounter rough going farther down the Columbia, but even the most accurate accounts could not prepare them for the difficulties to come. Beginning on October 23, 1805, the Corps entered a 55-mile stretch of the Columbia that constituted the most treacherous river passage of the entire trip. Here, as the powerful Columbia roared between volcanic rock, cutting its way through the Cascade Range in its descent to the sea, a succession of falls and rapids had been created. The first such passage, the Celilo (or Great) Falls, was negotiated by means of a short, comparatively easy portage, but immediately below the falls was The Dalles, as later travelers named it, comprising two stretches where the river was compressed between towering basalt cliffs, increasing its volume and power—the Short and Long Narrows, as Lewis and Clark named them. No portage was possible, and despite the "horrid appearance of this agitated gut Swelling, boiling & whorling," as Clark described it, the party was forced to run the rapids in their unwieldy dugouts. The local Indians, who used their own specially designed crafts to negotiate rough water, were astonished at the explorers' audacity.

After running the rapids, the Corps took time to rest and regroup at a site the captains called Fort Rock. Because

The Irish-born Canadian artist Paul Kane completed this painting, Mount Saint Helens Erupting, *in 1848. Lewis and Clark were not the first Americans to reach the Columbia; Robert Gray, a New England trader who discovered the river from the Pacific in 1792, named it after his ship. Mount Saint Helens was discovered and named later that same year by W. R. Broughton, a member of British navigator George Vancouver's expedition.*

the area's rapids and falls slowed the upstream movement of spawning salmon, the spot had become a favorite fishing ground for local Indians, which made it a perfect site for the captains to observe Indian life. Over time, The Dalles had become a market center controlled by the Wishram and Wasco Indians, whose houses lined the banks. Clark called it "the Great Mart of all this Country." The Wishram-Wasco plank-house villages served as the region's entrepôt for river-traffic trade goods, from where Pacific Northwest goods found their way up the Columbia to meet merchandise relayed from the Middle Missouri by Shoshone traders.

After a few days at Fort Rock camp, the party took on the final barrier, the Cascades, or Grand Rapids, which they negotiated on November 1–2. After the Cascades, the river broadened and slowed, and the topography and climate changed once again. Arid plains and stunted, twisted scrub pines and oaks gave way to lush forests of tremendous Douglas firs, red cedars, spruce, and hemlock. Rain regularly drenched the explorers. (Average annual rainfall on this part of the Columbia is 65 inches a year; on the plain it is less than 14 inches.) Near the mouth of the Willamette River, the Corps entered previously explored regions, for boats of George Vancouver's British expedition had come this far up the Columbia in 1792. To the north and south they noticed snow-peaked mountains, some named by Vancouver's party, including Mount Hood, Mount Saint Helens, and Mount Rainier. Clark could now check the accuracy of Vancouver's maps, copies of which he carried with him, and add firsthand observations to his own charts.

Evidences of European contact became more apparent as the party moved on; the men saw Indians wearing pieces of sailor's clothing and heard them using English words, mostly oaths and profanity. On November 7, the broad Columbia estuary opened before them, and Clark penned triumphantly, if a trifle prematurely, "Ocian in View! O! the joy." As the Corps worked its way along the northern side of the estuary, the men carved their names on trees to mark their triumphant transcontinental crossing. In imitative tribute to Alexander Mackenzie, Clark etched these words on a large pine: "William Clark December 3rd 1805. By Land from the U. States in 1804 & 1805."

Once past the rapids, the Corps of Discovery entered a "fertill and handsom" region, made intermittently disagreeable to Clark by heavy rainfall and the nocturnal, "horid" racket emitted by large numbers of ducks, geese, and swans. Clark was surprised to find that some of the Indians in the region wore sailor shirts and caps obtained in trade with the crews of merchant ships.

Winter on the Pacific

These people [Chinook and Clatsop] . . . have been very friendly to us; they appear to be a mild inoffensive people but will pilfer if they have an opportunity. . . . they are great higlers in trade.

They are generally low in stature, porportionably small, reather lighter complected and much more illy formed than the Indians of the Missouri.
                        —Meriwether Lewis, January 4 and 6, 1806

The party's understandable elation at reaching the Pacific was tempered by the miserable weather it found on its shores. Torrential rains fell often, and fog frequently blanketed the landscape. After two outposts proved unsatisfactory, the captains polled their party as to where a permanent winter encampment should be established. Even York and Sacagawea were allowed a vote. (Old Toby and the Nez Percé guides had left the party while it was still upriver on the Columbia.) Rather than retreat up the Columbia to drier ground, the Corps voted to cross to the south side of the estuary and seek a site with adequate timber and game for a winter headquarters. Fort Clatsop, named after the local Indians, was built on the Netul (known today as the Lewis and Clark) River, a short distance from present-day Astoria, Oregon—4,118 miles from Camp Dubois by the captains' estimate. Constructed from "the streight butifull balsom pine," according to

Kane's painting of a Chinook woman and her infant shows the mechanism used by the Indians of the Northwest to obtain the elongated foreheads that led to their being collectively known as Flatheads. The captains did not much care for the coast Indians, whom they characterized as dirty, physically unattractive, and thieving.

Clark, the stockade formed an enclosed square. Each of its walls was 50 feet in length. Two rows of rooms faced each other from the east and west end, across a 20-foot-wide parade ground. There were seven rooms in all. The captains shared the largest one and Charbonneau's family another; two were used for storing supplies, and the rest of the men crowded into the remaining three.

The basic purpose of the stockade was probably quite similar to Fort Mandan, but the Corps seems not to have enjoyed its stay on the coast as much as it did its winter on the plains. Part of the reason was the weather, which was unfailingly dreary and wet, but equally important was the explorers' distaste for the Indians of the region. Indeed, the captains' journals fail to conceal a certain sense of disgust with the inhabitants of the region, whom Lewis and Clark found greedy, untrustworthy, and generally less

The interior of a Chinook lodge. Among the few aspects of coast Indian life the captains admired was the quality of the furs the Indians used for their robes. Still, Lewis deplored how inadequate these robes were as clothing, particularly for the women. "I think the most disgusting thing I ever beheld is these dirty naked wenches," he wrote.

appealing than the Mandan, Hidatsa, Shoshone, and Nez
Percé. For more than 10 years, these Indians, the Chinook
and Clatsop, had been dealing with sea captains drawn to
the region to obtain sea otters for their fur. This experience
had accustomed them to driving a hard bargain, but the
men of the Corps often found their asking prices for goods,
particularly food, unreasonable. What the Indians viewed
as good business, the whites viewed as unconscionable
price gouging, particularly in light of their own growing
shortness of provisions and the generosity of tribes encountered earlier. The situation was aggravated by the fact
that the Corps was very low on the trade item the Indians
most desired—blue beads. That both tribes commonly engaged in petty thievery, as had some of the Columbia River
Indians, did not help relations. The men of the Corps
found the Clatsop, who lived on the south side of the
Columbia estuary, generally more agreeable, but they had
little use for the Chinook, who lived on the north side of
the bay. Absolutely no Indians were allowed to remain in
the fortress after sundown, which had not been the case
at Fort Mandan.

For these reasons, and also because U.S. interests were
less clearly defined here—the region along the Columbia
River was outside of the Louisiana Territory, and no nation
had a clear claim to it—the captains seem not to have
arranged any of their usual councils. The dwindling supply
of provisions, which would be needed for trading rather
than gift giving, also no doubt contributed to their decision. The enlisted men were more successful in establish-
ing relations of a different kind. A number of sexual
liaisons with Indian women took place, despite the captains' active discouragement because of the threat of venereal disease. A disapproving Lewis wrote of the Chinook,
"they do not hold the virtue of their women in high es-
timation, and will even prostitute their wives and daughters
for a fishinghook or stran of beads." His pique can be seen
as evidence of his general dissatisfaction at Fort Clatsop;

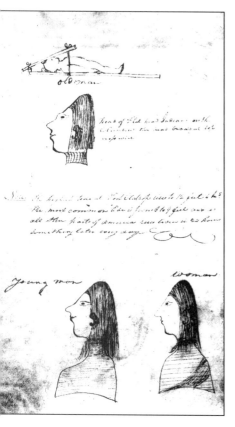

Clark's sketch of the characteristic elongated forehead of the coast Indians and the device used to obtain this effect. The contraption was usually used on infants for the first 10 or 12 months of life, longer on females than on males. Lewis and later observers believed that the process was essentially painless.

he had been much more tolerant of the liberated sexual practices of the Mandan, for example. Eventually, he was able to extract a sort of group vow of celibacy from his men.

The Indian practice of head deformation was observed with a good deal more acceptance. It was the custom of the coastal tribes, while their children were in infancy, to place them in special cradles equipped with a board that pressed against the forehead. Over time the pressure of the board brought about the desired effect, a nearly straight slope of the forehead from the top of the skull to the nose, yielding a pointed look when viewed from the side and a flattened appearance when seen from the front. Clark drew pictures of the cradle and the result of its work in his journal. The look was considered a mark of status, which nonmembers of the tribe were not permitted to imitate.

One aspect of Indian culture that the captains did devote considerable attention to was the natives' inventive use of local plant resources. Roots played important roles in the Indian diet, including edible thistle (which the captains called *shannetahque* after the Indian word), western bracken fern, rushes, cattail, seashore lupine, and most importantly, wapatoo. Wapatoo was not indigenous to the Fort Clatsop area but was acquired farther up the Columbia. It grew in swampy places and was harvested by women who waded into the water, pulled the bulbs loose with their feet, and tossed the floating plants into canoes. The roots were usually cooked, either by boiling or roasting, but sometimes were eaten raw. Accustomed to a diet of buffalo, deer, and elk, Lewis characterized the taste of wapatoo as "reather insipid." Fruits and berries were also important to the native diet, including a plant new to science, salal, whose purple berries were pulverized and made into loaves or else boiled to make a soup.

Fish was the most important staple of the Indians' diet, however. The Columbia provided sturgeon, eulachon, trout, and most important of all, several varieties of salmon. The coastal Indians were extremely creative fishermen, and the captains described in great detail their methods and equipment, including their skillful handling of their graceful, finely crafted canoes. The captains' interest in Indian methods of subsistence may have been stimulated by their own concern with the Corps' ability to last out the winter. Although game was not exactly scarce, it was nowhere near as abundant as it had been on the Great Plains, and the expedition's hunters often ranged far afield in their search for meat, sometimes elk but more often deer or smaller animals, such as birds. Lewis's journal entries betray his frequent worry that his men were using food wastefully and that there would not be enough to last the winter, and several times he scolded them for their profligate ways. On those days when the hunters were successful, his enjoyment is palpable. "This evening we

Miller's sketch of Indians gathering roots. Lewis was impressed by the authority that Clatsop and Chinook women exercised in their households; he theorized that the relative equality of men and women in coast Indian culture existed because women participated equally with the men in providing food for the family, as opposed to the more hunting-oriented tribes of the Great Plains.

had what I call an excellent supper it consisted of a mar-rowbone a piece and a brisket of boiled Elk . . . this for Fort Clatsop is living in high stile," he wrote on one such occasion. On New Year's Day, 1806, he wrote of his longing for that day, perhaps a year hence, when he and the rest of the men would again find themselves "in the bosom of our friends . . . [to] enjoy the repast which the hand of civilization has prepared for us."

Overall, most of the winter was spent in the routine of providing for day-to-day needs and preparing for the re-sumption of the journey. For the enlisted men, this largely meant cleaning and repairing equipment. For skilled out-doorsmen such as Colter and Drouillard, it meant frequent hunting trips. Joseph Field fashioned furniture, including a crude desk for the captains' use. York handled much of the cooking. Bratton, Gibson, and Joseph Field established a camp about 15 miles southwest of Fort Clatsop, along the Pacific Coast, where rotating teams of 3 or 4 men went to boil down seawater for salt, which was necessary to preserve meat and make more palatable the diet of roots, herbs, dried fish, and dog meat on which the Corps sub-sisted when other food was not available. All the men

While Lewis was writing and polishing his journal notes in the winter of 1805–6, Clark worked on his maps of the West. This detail charts the Corps' portage around the Great Falls of the Columbia.

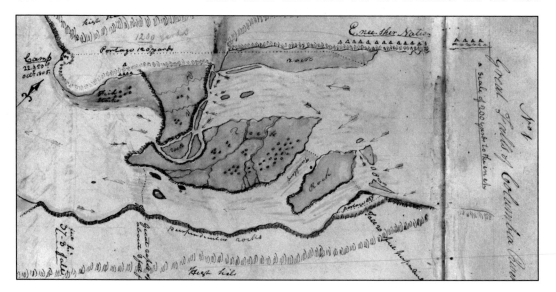

spent much time making new clothes out of elk skin for the return trip. The captains reported that by the end of winter the men had made 338 pairs of moccasins and an unspecified amount of leather pants and shirts.

Lewis spent much of his time writing, Clark mapmaking. Perhaps because of his enforced leisure, Lewis now completed his most extensive and detailed writing of the entire trip, most of it concerned with descriptions of flora, fauna, and the Indians encountered since reaching the Rocky Mountains, a period of time during which Lewis's entries had been sporadic. Among the plant species that Lewis described at this time are the Oregon crab apple, the Oregon and dull Oregon grapes, and salal, all of which he also sketched. He also devoted a considerable amount of space to describing the great conifers of the region, such as the Sitka spruce, the grand fir, the Douglas fir, and the western white pine. The new animals he noted—some of his most descriptive writing—include the Columbian black-tailed deer, the mountain beaver (a gopherlike rodent), the Oregon bobcat, the greater white-fronted goose, the northern fulmar (a seabird), the whistling swan, the eulachon (or smelt), and the steelhead trout. In order to provide this material with a better chance of reaching Jefferson safely, Clark copied all of it into his own journals. He also worked together with Lewis compiling an elaborate document entitled "Estimate of Western Indians" (that is, those Indians west of the Rocky Mountains), a counterpart to the similar study completed at Fort Mandan for Eastern tribes. This new table listed tribal names, numbers, and locations, but did not include as extensive material about customs, beliefs, and behavior. Nevertheless, in their journals both men gave careful attention to native clothing, houses, utensils, weapons, and implements, and they wrote general descriptions of coastal material culture.

Clark's most important work during the winter months consisted of his preparation of maps of the route west from Fort Mandan. In his journals, Clark had drawn numerous

This drawing and description of the coho, or silver salmon, was part of Lewis's journal entry for Sunday, March 16, 1806. Lewis called the fish the "white Salmon Trout."

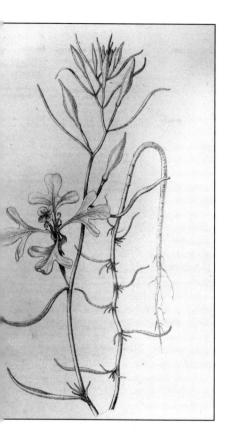

maps of this territory, and he augmented these with larger, more detailed sheets. At Fort Clatsop, he completed a large map of the country west of the Missouri River. These route charts and the great map of the West depended both on Clark's firsthand experience and on information gathered from the Indians. Clark's maps were extremely accurate concerning the regions the Corps of Discovery had traversed, less so for areas that he had only heard about, but taken all in all they constituted the most complete and accurate cartographic account of the West to that point.

Despite these labors, the winter passed slowly for all the men, although there were a few diversions. Christmas was celebrated with singing and dancing and the exchange of gifts. The captains gave the last of the tobacco to those who used it, and a silk handkerchief to those who did not. Clark appreciatively recorded the gifts he received— woolen clothing from Lewis, moccasins from Whitehouse, an Indian basket from Silas Goodrich, and two dozen white weasel tails from Sacagawea. Ordway lamented the lack of liquor for toasting but observed that "all are in good health which we esteem more than all the ardent Spirits in the world." A week later, the new year was wrung in with a rifle salute fired into the air. Later in January, Clark led a detachment of 13 men as well as Sacagawea and little Jean Baptiste to view the monstrous carcass of a whale stranded on the beach south of the salt-making camp. The local Indians sold him a few hundred pounds of whale meat and several gallons of oil.

But such diversions were few and far between, and boredom, the monotonous diet, widespread illness (the usual afflictions common to a group sharing common quarters in a cold, damp climate), and unceasing miserable weather increased the Corps' impatience to set out for home. There were practical reasons for wishing to move on as well. The Corps had accomplished a great deal, as much if not more than anyone had expected, but their business would not be complete until they passed on their findings to Jefferson.

The captains had hoped to send some of their material back East aboard one of the ships that the Indians said were in the habit of calling at the Columbia, but none arrived during the winter of 1805–6. They had also decided to carry out some further exploration on the return journey—a reconnaissance of the Yellowstone River and a search for a more direct route from the Rockies to the Great Falls region of the Missouri—and were anxious to begin. Furthermore, the Corps wished to retrieve their horses from the Nez Percé before the Indians set out over the mountains for their spring buffalo hunt.

The captains set April 1 as a departure date, but as March dragged drearily along, the eagerness of all to be under way rendered Fort Clatsop uninhabitable, and the date was moved up. Only three dugouts had survived the winter; the captains were eager to purchase two of the Clatsop's nimble vessels but believed the asking price to be too severe in light of their dwindling stock of provisions. (The Indians prized their boats greatly; according to Lewis, a good canoe was the customary price for a girl's hand in marriage.) Drouillard came up with a solution by persuading an Indian to hand one over in exchange for Lewis's laced uniform coat. That left the Corps one short, a problem the captains solved by authorizing Drouillard to steal one. They apparently rationalized this singular departure from strict policy by noting that the Clatsop had earlier that winter stolen the carcasses of six elk killed by the Corps' hunters.

On March 20, Lewis penned a reflective passage on the winter's stay: "Altho' we have not fared sumptuously this winter and spring at Fort Clatsop, we have lived quite as comfortably as we have any reason to expect we should; and have accomplished every object which induced our remaining at this place except that of meeting with the traders who visit the entrance of this river." Two days later, his tone had grown more urgent: "We determined to set out tomorrow at all events," he wrote.

Two of the botanical specimens discovered by Lewis: the Clarkia pulchella *(left), a perennial herb, known also as ragged robin, that was named after Clark; and the salmonberry (above), a red-flowered raspberry he described as a "large leafed thorn."*

The Way Home

the rained seased and it became fair about Meridian, at
which time we loaded our canoes & at 1 P. M. left Fort
Clatsop on our homeward bound journey. at this place we
had wintered and remained from the 7th of Decr. 1805 to
this day and have lived as well as we had any right to
expect.

—William Clark, March 23, 1806

Because on the early part of its return journey the Corps
retraced its previous year's route, the captains did not
bother to make detailed records of courses and distances,
although Clark made constant improvements to his maps
and the men still filled their journals with incidents of the
voyage and descriptions of the country and its people.
There were new discoveries to be made as well. On April
6, near Beacon Rock in present-day Washington, Reuben
Field brought in a bird that Lewis thought resembled the
Virginia quail or bobwhite. It was the beautiful mountain
quail; because of his lengthy and accurate description,
Lewis can be given credit for its discovery.

Clark's geographical interest required the party to stop
in the area of today's Portland, Oregon, in order to seek
a river that had begun to figure prominently in the captains' conception of western geography. The Indians called
it the Multnomah, a name adopted by the captains; today
it is known as the Willamette River. The Corps had missed
it on the downriver trip, but on the return journey Clark
and a small group, aided by an Indian guide, carried out

Miller's portrait of a Nez Percé Indian. Clark described the members of the tribe as "stout likely men, handsom women, and very dressey in their way." The men generally wore a "White Buffalow robe or Elk Skin dressed with beeds," with "sea shells & the Mother of Pirl" in their hair and around their neck and white, green, or light blue pants "which they find in their Countrey."

a brief reconnaissance on April 2 and 3 while the main party camped on the Columbia's north shore. Clark's sojourn was not extensive enough to provide him with clear information on the length and course of the Willamette—on his maps, he confused its course with that of the Snake, which the Indians had also told him about, and he incorrectly had it originating far in the interior of the continent—but the captains were correct in their assessment of the "Columbian valley," the area between the Cascade and Coast ranges. Lewis declared it "the only desirable situation for a settlement which I have seen on the West side of the Rocky mountains," capable of supporting 50,000 persons. Based partly on Lewis's description, the Willamette Valley became the focal point for Oregon emigrants in the 1840s and today supports a much greater population than Lewis could ever have imagined.

On April 6 the party was again on its way. It took nearly two weeks to get upriver past the Cascades and the Celilo Falls. The portage was again wearisome, and relations with Indians in the vicinity continued to be poor. Hunting provided insufficient food for the men, so the explorers again had to obtain dogs, dried fish, and roots from the river tribes. The Indians were also feeling hunger's pinch, as the spring salmon run was late, and they demanded high prices. Some also could not resist a little thievery. The captains' patience was at low ebb, and they threatened violence if stolen goods were not returned. Clark wrote that he informed the Indians "that I had it in my power at that moment to kill them all and set fire to their houses, but it was not my wish to treat them with severity provided they would let my property alone." An exasperated Lewis declared the river Indians "poor, dirty, proud, haughty, inhospitable, parsimonious and faithless in every rispect." When some Indians made off with Seaman, the captain sent a party of men to recover his dog, with orders to shoot if necessary. Fortunately, no one was killed and Seaman was returned. Sergeant Gass probably summed up the enlisted men's opinion: "All the Indians from the Rocky Mountains to the falls of Columbia, are an honest, ingenious and well disposed people; but from the falls to the seacoast, and along it, they are a rascally, thieving set."

Past the falls, the Corps purchased horses and traded their canoes for beads. The journey now continued by land along the north side of the Columbia. Fulfilling a promise the captains made on the westward journey, the Corps accepted the hospitality of Chief Yelleppit of the Walula (or Wallawalla) and camped with him and his people from April 27–29 at the mouth of the Walla Walla River. In addition to ferrying the whites, their provisions, and their horses to the south side of the river, Yelleppit

For the return journey the Corps procured two intricately carved Indian canoes like the ones shown here—one through barter, the other by theft. While passing a Cathlamet village on the Columbia, the Corps was confronted by an Indian who claimed the stolen vessel was his. "Having no time to discuss the question of right," Sergeant Patrick Gass wrote, "we compromised with him for an elk skin."

provided much-needed food and entertained the expedition with a lavish feast at which Cruzatte played his fiddle, Indian musicians drummed, and the whites and the Indians danced together until early in the morning. When the whites departed, the Walula sold them several horses—the Corps' herd now numbered 23—and Yelleppit presented Clark an "eligant" white steed and told the captains about an overland shortcut to the Nez Percé. Lewis called the Walula "the most hospitable, honest, and sincere people that we have met with in our voyage." Using the new route, the Corps reached the Clearwater from the Columbia in six days, following Indian trails and the Touchet River and circumventing the Snake almost entirely, then proceeded southeast along the Clearwater in search of the Nez Percé villages. On May 14 the party camped on the east side of the Clearwater, at the site of the future town of Kamiah, Idaho, where, to Lewis's increasing frustration, they would remain for nearly a month. It may have been springtime in the valley, but as the Nez Percé let the captains know, it was still winter in the mountains and it would be several weeks before the snows in the Bitterroots melted sufficiently to allow passage over the Lolo Trail. An impatient Lewis wrote of "that icy barrier which separates us from my friends and country, from all which makes life esteemable."

At Camp Chopunnish, the men passed their time seeking food, counseling and socializing with the Indians, and obtaining more horses for the next stage of the trip. The captains assumed a demanding role as physicians to the Indians. On the westward trip some expedition prescriptions had eased Indian ailments and, Clark wrote, "given those nativs an exolted oppinion of my skill as a phisician." In the spring of 1806, Clark became the natives' "favorite phisician," according to Lewis. During his stay the captain was visited by a host of afflicted persons complaining of a variety of ills, notably rheumatic problems, sore eyes, and abscesses. Lewis was doubtful if any permanent cures were

Hunters blast away at a fleeing elk. Keeping the Corps in meat was a constant challenge for its hunters. Gass recorded that during its residence at Fort Clatsop, for example, the Corps killed 131 elks. The animals were more than just food sources; their skin was used to make clothing and moccasins and to exchange with the Indians. Some of the captains' journals were even bound in elk skin.

possible for these "poor wretches," but the immediate benefits were good relations with the Nez Percé, including payment in food stuffs.

As always, the captains also used their time to study local geography and natural history. Clark gathered information about the country and tribes to the north and south and later updated his master map based on this intelligence. His maps from the Nez Percé comprise some of the finest pieces of Indian cartography obtained on the expedition. Lewis refined his evaluation of the grizzly bear, concluding that despite the different colors of the bears he had seen—a grizzly may have yellowish, reddish, or even black fur—they were all of the same species. His final words on *Ursus horribilis* were penned somewhat later: "These bear are a most tremenduous animal; it seems that the hand of providence has been most wonderfully in our

Bodmer's Chasing off the Grizzlies. *The ferocity of these "gentlemen," as Lewis referred to the great bears, astonished all who visited the West, but their once vast domain would steadily diminish as American civilization expanded westward.*

Even before their encounter with Lewis, the Blackfeet had earned a reputation for intransigence and warlike behavior. They had driven the Shoshone and Nez Percé into the mountains, and French traders called them mauvais sujets, *or bad subjects. On July 16, 1806, Lewis wrote, "As they are a viciouis lawless and reather an abandoned set of wretches I wish to avoid an interview with them if possible."*

favor with rispect to them or some of us would long since have fallen a sacrifice to their farosity." It was Lewis who gave them the name *grizzly*, because of the grizzled appearance of their fur, which tends to get lighter near the tips. Lewis also took this time to describe a number of new animals and plants, including the western horned toad, Columbian ground squirrel, western tanager, mariposa lily, bear grass, and ragged robin (named scientifically for Clark).

As elsewhere, at Camp Chopunnish the captains devoted much time and energy to Indian diplomacy. They successfully mediated a dispute between some squabbling Nez Percé chiefs, and in councils they repeated their promise, first uttered the previous year, that American merchants would soon visit the area with trade goods, especially guns, so the Nez Percé could defend themselves against the Blackfeet and other enemies. They also promised, if they should meet the Blackfeet on their eastward trip, to try to persuade them to make peace with the Nez Percé. For the most part, relations between the whites and

the Nez Percé were excellent, although there was a brief altercation between Lewis and an Indian who interrupted the captain's supper of dog meat by tossing a puppy at him. The Nez Percé did not eat dog, and the toss was no doubt Indian commentary on the whites' culinary tastes. Lewis flung the poor puppy back at the Indian and menacingly brandished his tomahawk, but peace was soon restored. Overall, however, the captains found much to admire about the Nez Percé and their way of life, and they devoted many pages in their journals to their observations about the Nez Percé culture.

According to the Indians, the Lolo Trail would not be clear of snow until the beginning of July, but because the entire Corps was anxious to start homeward, the party left the Clearwater Valley for the mountains on June 10, "ex-olted," Clark wrote, "with the idea of once more proceeding on towards their friends and Country." But after a week's travel, deep snow prevented the Corps from continuing on, and for the first time it was forced to turn back. Lewis lamented, "this is the first time since we have been on this long tour that we have ever been compelled to retreat."

On June 24 the Corps set out again, this time accompanied by three Nez Percé guides who had agreed to take the expedition as far as the Great Falls in exchange for two rifles. The Indians easily found the way to the Lolo Trail, which this time took the men only six days to traverse, with no repetition of previous hardships. The expedition again paused to regroup at Travelers Rest, where the captains finalized plans, first devised at Fort Clatsop, to split their command in two so as to investigate previously unexplored territory. A rendezvous was set for the mouth of the Yellowstone River on the Missouri. On July 3, the two groups went their separate ways. It was the first time during the expedition that the command had been permanently divided, and Lewis admitted that he "could not avoid feeling much concern on this occasion."

Reunion and Return

> I called to them as I had done several times before that I
> would shoot them if they did not give me my horse . . .
> one of them jumped behind a rock and . . . the other
> turned around . . . and I shot him through the belly, he
> fell to his knees and . . . fired at me . . . being
> bearheaded I felt the wind of his bullet very distinctly.
> —Meriwether Lewis, July 27, 1806

The captains knew now that their outbound route, following the twisting Missouri to its headwaters, had been needlessly roundabout and that there were trails across the mountains that would shorten the journey considerably. This quicker route needed to be examined. Moreover, they wished to discover the northernmost reach of the Marias River, in the hope of expanding U.S. claims under the Louisiana Purchase. Consequently, Lewis would investigate the shortcut by heading northeast to the Great Falls, then explore the Marias before returning to the Missouri. Clark's mission was to explore the Yellowstone River. He would travel southeast to the site of Camp Fortunate, then follow the Beaverhead and the Jefferson rivers to the Three Forks of the Missouri. Part of his group would then take canoes down the Missouri to the Great Falls to meet Lewis's party there, while Clark and selected others went overland to the Yellowstone. The scattered groups would eventually recombine where the Yellowstone entered the Missouri.

Bodmer's portrayal of an Arikara warrior. On their return voyage, Lewis and Clark learned that the peace they had attempted to arrange between the Arikara and the Mandan and Hidatsa had broken down and that the Arikara chief who had gone to visit Jefferson in Washington, D.C., had died there.

The two divisions set out from Travelers Rest on July 3, 1805. Lewis was accompanied by nine men, volunteers for what was considered the more dangerous assignment, and five Nez Percé guides who left the detachment the next day. With its 17 horses the party moved north down the Bitterroot River to the vicinity of present-day Missoula, Montana, then east across the Continental Divide following the Clark Fork and Big Blackfoot rivers on a route previously recommended by the mountain Indians. Along the way the captain's dog Seaman was honored, as other members of the Corps had been, by having a small stream named for him; today it is Monture Creek in Montana. Eventually, Lewis and his men crossed the divide over what is now called Lewis and Clark Pass, although Clark never saw it.

A Piegan Blackfeet encampment, based on a painting by Bodmer. The Blackfeet recognized immediately that the arrival of American traders on the upper Missouri would permanently alter the balance of power in the region to their detriment.

By July 13 they had reached the old Upper Portage
Camp above the Great Falls. It had taken 11 days to reach
this spot from Travelers Rest; the previous year it had taken
the Corps nearly 2 months of hard traveling to traverse
the territory between those 2 points. The new route was
also 600 miles shorter. After months of meager rations,
the soldiers were delighted to be able to eat buffalo again.
Lewis was amazed that "there were not less than 10 thousand buffaloe within a circle of 2 miles" about the place.
Unfortunately, large numbers of grizzlies also called the
region home, and many prowled menacingly around the
camp as the men dug up the cache of supplies they had
buried the previous year. Hugh McNeal had a close call
when his horse almost rode over a concealed bear. The
horse reared and threw him, and McNeal broke his mis-
firing musket over the beast's head and then spent several
hours in a tree waiting for the stunned and angry bear to
leave.

Because of the loss of several horses, perhaps to Indian
thieves, Lewis decided to take only three of his best men
to the Marias—Drouillard and the Field brothers. Sergeant Gass and the others would await the canoe party
from Clark's detachment, then all would portage the Great
Falls, recover additional supplies buried there, and proceed to the mouth of the Marias to meet the returning
Lewis and his detachment. If the rendezvous at the Marias
did not take place by September 1, Gass was to move on
and join Clark at the Yellowstone.

To Lewis's disappointment, the reconnaissance along
the Marias, which lasted from July 16 to July 26, proved
that the river did not extend as far north as he had hoped.
On July 26, in the vicinity of Two Medicine Creek, Lewis
and his men encountered eight Blackfeet Indians of the
Piegan tribe. Well armed with guns obtained from Canadian traders, the Blackfeet were the one tribe Lewis had
been trying to avoid, for he was well aware that they were
the avowed enemies of the Indians—the Shoshone and

the Nez Percé—the Corps had befriended. But having been spotted, he believed a retreat would be foolish. He did not want the Indians to believe that he was afraid of them, and as they were accompanied by a herd of 30 horses, he believed that other Blackfeet might be concealed nearby, ready to cut off his withdrawal. Instead, the two groups advanced toward one another. When they met, Lewis, using sign language, gave the Indians his usual council speech and invited them to come with him to the mouth of the Marias to meet his other men and see his large boat with its mounted gun. The Indians were non-committal; that night, the two groups camped together on Two Medicine Creek. The next morning the explorers were awakened by the noise of a struggle; one of the Indians had tried to make off with some of the party's rifles. Joseph Field, the early morning guard, quickly awakened his brother Reuben, who pursued the Piegan and stabbed him to death. Another Indian seized the rifles of Drouillard and Lewis, but Drouillard saw him and wrested back his own gun. His shouts and struggles aroused Lewis, who grabbed his pistol and pursued an Indian fleeing with his rifle. He caught the thief, and with pistol at ready ordered him to lay down the rifle. When the Indian did so, Lewis allowed him to go.

Having failed to obtain the explorers' guns, the Blackfeet now tried to steal their horses. Lewis ran after two of the rustlers; when one Indian turned to fire at him, Lewis shot first, hitting the man in the stomach. The fatally wounded warrior fired a final shot that passed closely by Lewis's scalp. The six surviving Piegans fled north, while Lewis and his men quickly gathered up their belongings and began two days of hard riding back to the Missouri, spurred on by fear of avenging Blackfeet warriors. At the mouth of the Marias they met Sergeant Ordway, who had picked up the men Lewis had left at the Great Falls. In five canoes and the white pirogue, the whole party easily outdistanced any potential pursuers.

Meanwhile, Clark's trip on the Yellowstone proceeded a good deal less dramatically. After departing Travelers' Rest on July 3, he and his men proceeded south along the Bitterroot Valley, crossed the Continental Divide at Gibbon's Pass, and, directed by Sacagawea, followed buffalo and Indian trails through the Big Hole River Valley to Camp Fortunate. After retrieving supplies left there the previous year—tobacco was especially appreciated—the explorers journeyed by horse and canoe down to the Three Forks. The same journey the summer before had taken three weeks; now it took three days. They arrived on July 13, just as Lewis reached the Upper Portage Camp, some

White wolves rest on the bluffs towering above the upper Missouri in this painting by Catlin. "I have no doubt but this tract of country if cultivated would produce in great abundance every article essentially necessary to the comfort and subsistence of civilized man," Lewis wrote on the return journey.

George Caleb Bingham's classic
Fur Traders Descending the
Missouri. *Lewis and Clark's
return marked the beginning of a
new era in American history:
When the explorers met up with
the fur traders William Dickson
and Joseph Hancock, who were
looking for a guide upriver, John
Colter agreed to go with them,
launching the age of the
mountain men.*

150 miles to the north. That same day, Clark divided his party, sending Ordway with 9 men down the Missouri in canoes to meet the Gass contingent, while he led a party of 12 persons, including the Charbonneau family, by land east to the Yellowstone.

Clark and his group traveled through the valleys of the Gallatin and East Gallatin rivers, a landscape filled with enormous herds of deer, elk, and antelope in all directions and with great numbers of beaver in the rivers. Following well-worn but confusing Indian trails, again pointed out by Sacagawea—Clark remarked that she had been of great service "as a pilot through this country"—the party moved through Bozeman Pass and crossed to the Yellowstone on July 15. On the north side of the Yellowstone, near present-day Laurel, Montana, the party stopped to build canoes from cottonwood trees. While the boat builders were at work, Indian bandits—probably Crow—made off with 24 of the party's 50 mounts.

On July 24, Clark decided to split his unit once more. He sent an advance party under Sergeant Pryor with the remaining horses cross-country to the Mandan villages to deliver a message to a Canadian trader, asking him to induce some Teton Sioux chiefs to go to Washington with the captains. Shortly after Pryor and his three companions set out, their horses were stolen, again perhaps by stealthy Crow. Pryor handled the emergency admirably. His party killed some buffalo and used the hides to build bowl-shaped "bull boats" such as they had observed used by Missouri River tribes. They then set off down the Yellowstone in pursuit of Clark's party, whom they overtook on August 8.

Clark's trip down the Yellowstone was largely uneventful, notable mainly for the almost frenzied hunting done by himself and the other men. Wildlife in the region was unbelievably abundant; at night, Clark feared that his men would be trampled by the passing herds of buffalo, and the grunting and snorting of the beasts nearby played havoc with the men's sleep. At times, the party had to wait on the riverbank while herds miles long crossed ahead of them. Elk were almost as numerous, and the men hunted gleefully, out of joy in the killing as much as any necessity. On July 25, near today's Billings, Montana, Clark carved his name and the date on the butte he named Pompy's Tower after little Jean Baptiste; it is now called Pompey's Pillar. Hurrying onward, he reached the Missouri on August 3, then proceeded a little downriver after leaving a note for Lewis. His counterpart arrived at the mouth of the Yellowstone on August 7, read Clark's message, and moved on, only to be laid low four days later by a painful and embarrassing accident. While out hunting, Cruzatte, who had poor eyesight, fired at a movement in the grass he took to be an elk, only to discover that he had shot his buckskin-clad commanding officer in the left buttock. Although not life threatening, the wound was quite painful and disabling. Ever the naturalist, on August 12, Lewis found energy to describe one last plant, the pin cherry, before he laid down his pen. On that same day, a few miles below the Little Knife River in present-day North Dakota, Lewis and Clark reunited. Clark assumed the remaining writing duties for his ailing comrade.

The full party reached the Mandan and Hidatsa villages two days later. The usual gunfire salutes, exchanges of gifts, and councils took place, but during their three-day stay the captains were dismayed to learn of the failure of much of their early Indian diplomacy. Since their winter at Fort Mandan, the Hidatsa had attacked the Shoshone and Arikara, the Sioux had raided the Mandan and Hidatsa, and so on. Undaunted, Clark—Lewis was still unable to walk—persuaded the Mandan chief Big White (Sheheke) to accompany them to Washington to see the president. On its departure on August 17, the Corps of Discovery left behind Sacagawea, Charbonneau, and little Pomp. The Corps was also short one member, John Colter, who asked for his discharge in order to return to the wilderness with two fur trappers, William Dickson and Joseph Hancock, whom the expedition had encountered on the Missouri on August 11. The captains' tales of the great numbers of beaver to be found upriver had greatly excited these two gentlemen, who persuaded Colter to guide them. Thus began the career of one of the greatest of the mountain men. On August 18, Lewis celebrated his last birthday on the trail—his 32nd.

The remainder of the return journey was made quickly. A stop was made at the Arikara villages, a cool encounter took place with the Teton Sioux, a more cordial exchange with the Yankton Sioux occurred, and the Corps revisited Sergeant Floyd's grave. By the middle of September, Lewis was on his feet again—he even collected a new botanical specimen, the pink cleome—and meetings with trading parties headed upriver were becoming commonplace. From them, the captains learned that many people in the United States had given them up for lost, although, as Clark put it, "the President of the U. States had yet hopes of us." The traders also sold them some whiskey—the first spirits the Corps had enjoyed since July 4, 1805.

At noon on September 23, the Corps of Discovery entered St. Louis to the cheers of citizens lining the riverfront. Two days later, at Christy's Tavern, the men of the Corps

Chester Harding painted this full-length portrait of Clark in later life, during the time the captain served as superintendent of Indian affairs in St. Louis, which the Indians came to refer to as "Red Hair's town." As he had promised, Clark saw to the education of Sacagawea's son Jean Baptiste.

As the advance scouts of American civilization, Lewis and Clark were the harbingers of the inevitable destruction of the way of life of the western Indians. Catlin visited the Indians when that process was already well advanced. "I have seen him set fire to his wigwam and smooth over the graves of his fathers . . . clap his hand in silence over his mouth, and take the last look over his fair hunting ground, and turn his face in sadness to the setting sun," he wrote.

were treated to a lavish dinner, replete with 18 toasts, ending with "Captains Lewis and Clark—Their perilous services endear them to every American heart." The next day Clark brought his journal to an end with the anticlimactic words, "a fine morning we commenced wrighting &c."

So ended the Voyage of Discovery, justly acclaimed since as the most successful such venture ever sponsored by the United States. It is true that Lewis and Clark failed to discover an *easily* traversed route from the Missouri to the Pacific (for the very good reason that one does not exist), that some of their scientific, geographical, and ethnographic conclusions have since been demonstrated as incorrect, and that their efforts at Indian diplomacy were soon afterward largely undone; but their myriad successes more than outweigh these petty failures. Lewis and Clark provided the United States with the first comprehensive look at the magnificent western lands on its doorstep. Although Clark was not a trained cartographer, his renowned

great map of the West, which was first published in 1814, was among the most influential ever created. His maps became invaluable to government officials, military men, engineers, settlers, fur traders, and future explorers, and in the years since they have been consistently praised for their content and their style. Although Lewis was not a trained naturalist, he introduced literally hundreds of new species of flora and fauna to the scientific and public consciousness. His exacting method and observant eye, not to mention his enthusiasm for his task, represent the essence of the scientific spirit of inquiry, even if they were the result of only haphazard scientific training. His descriptions are entertaining, detailed, meticulous, and accurate, and one cannot read Lewis's journal entries without being impressed by the zeal and skill with which he fulfilled his charge of recording his impressions of the strange new environments through which the Corps journeyed. Clark's appreciation for the landscape, wildlife, and peoples of the West was no less great.

The manner in which the expedition was conducted is every bit as important as its results. The Voyage of Discovery was a masterpiece of planning, improvisation, teamwork, and leadership rarely, if ever, equaled in the annals of exploration. In traversing thousands of miles of what, to white Americans, was a previously unexplored wilderness, Lewis and Clark and the Corps of Discovery lost only one man, to an illness that most likely even the most accomplished physicians of the day would have been unable to treat successfully. There were only minor incidents of petty insubordination, none of attempted mutiny. Faced with the countless challenges of travel and survival in an unknown and perilous environment, the captains and other members of the Corps achieved a rare harmony that enabled them to meet all of the voyage's challenges. This appreciation of the manner in which the expedition was conducted should extend to the Corps' relations with the native peoples of the West, which, except for one minor, unavoidable incident, were peaceful. That Lewis and Clark were the advance scouts for an inevitable westward expansion of the United States that would make future peaceful relations impossible does not detract from their own conduct, which reflected a genuine desire for amity between the two peoples. And while not entirely free of bias, the writings of the captains generally reveal an interest in and respect for the Indians as human beings that is admirable.

Clark lived for 32 years after the voyage's completion, Lewis for only 3. Clark had a successful career as superintendent of Indian Affairs for the United States; Lewis, a brief, unfortunate stint as governor of the Louisiana Territory. Clark married twice, the first time to Julia Hancock—the "Judith" for whom he named the Judith River—and fathered several children, the oldest of whom he named Meriwether Lewis. Lewis remained a bachelor; he was never able to begin composing the formal report on his adventures that Jefferson requested. When the responsibility became his, Clark turned the materials over to a ghostwriter; the work was not published until 1814. Engulfed in undefinable melancholia, Lewis resorted to drink. En route to Washington, D.C., in September 1809, he fatally shot himself, in a roadside tavern along the Natchez Trace in present-day Tennessee. A complete edition of the captains' journals was not published for the first time until the first decade of the 20th century; with their appearance grew a new appreciation for Lewis and Clark as scientists, cartographers, pioneers, and writers—the quintessential explorers, fascinated by all that they encountered in a new land. The journals remain America's national epic of exploration, a record of the first knowledge, according to Jefferson, who reflected the optimism of the young republic, of "that vast and fertile country, which their sons are destined to fill with arts, with science, with freedom and happiness."

The westernmost portion of Clark's great map of the West, which was finally published in 1814. Incredibly detailed, it fulfilled Jefferson's objectives of mapping the previously uncharted regions of the upper Missouri and Columbia rivers. In a very short time after its appearance, American settlements would begin to dot the vast landscape west of the Mississippi.

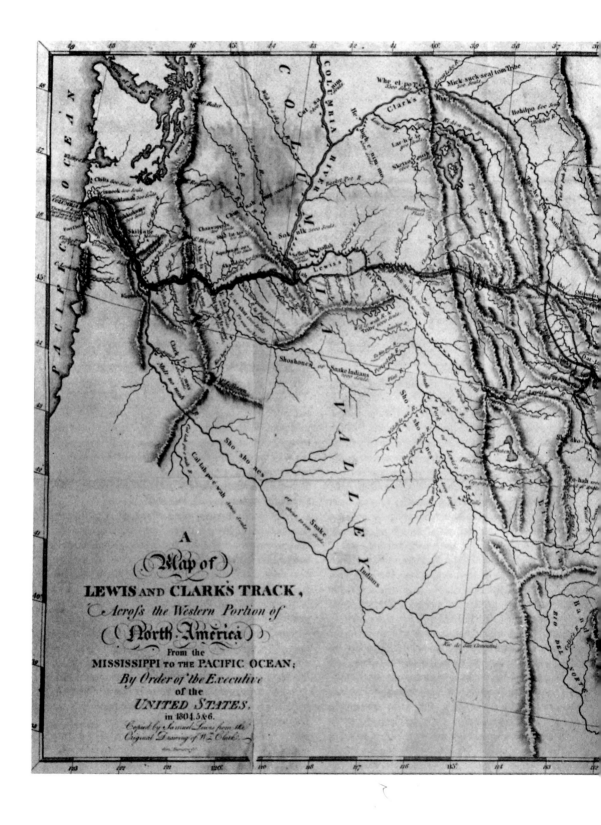

A
Map of
LEWIS AND CLARK'S TRACK,
Across the Western Portion of
North America
From the
MISSISSIPPI TO THE PACIFIC OCEAN;
By Order of the Executive
of the
UNITED STATES,
in 1804, 5 & 6.
Copied by Samuel Lewis from the
Original Drawing of W. Clark.

Further Reading

Allen, John Logan. *Passage Through the Garden: Lewis and Clark and the Image of the American Northwest.* Urbana: University of Illinois Press, 1975.

Bakeless, John. *Lewis and Clark, Partners in Discovery.* New York: Morrow, 1947.

Betts, Robert B. *In Search of York: The Slave Who Went to the Pacific with Lewis and Clark.* Boulder: Colorado Associated University Press, 1985.

Burroughs, Raymond Darwin. *The Natural History of the Lewis and Clark Expedition.* East Lansing: Michigan State University Press, 1961.

Charbonneau, Louis. *Trail: The Story of the Lewis and Clark Expedition.* Garden City, NY: Doubleday, 1989.

Chuinard, Eldon G. *Only One Man Died: The Medical Aspects of the Lewis and Clark Expedition.* Glendale, CA: Clark, 1979.

Dillon, Richard. *Meriwether Lewis: A Biography.* New York: Coward-McCann, 1965.

Duncan, Dayton. *Out West: An American Journey.* New York: Viking, 1987.

Eide, Ingvard Henry. *American Odyssey: The Journals of Lewis and Clark.* New York: Rand McNally, 1969.

Howard, Harold P. *Sacajawea.* Norman: University of Oklahoma Press, 1972.

Jackson, Donald, ed. *Letters of the Lewis and Clark Expedition with Related Documents, 1783–1854.* Vols. 1 and 2. Urbana: University of Illinois Press, 1978.

Lavender, David. *The Way to the Western Sea: Lewis and Clark Across the Continent.* New York: Harper & Row, 1988.

Moulton, Gary E., ed. *The Journals of the Lewis and Clark Expedition.* 11 vols. Lincoln: University of Nebraska Press, 1983–.

Ronda, James. *Lewis and Clark Among the Indians.* Lincoln: University of Nebraska Press, 1984.

Thwaites, Reuben Gold, ed. *Original Journals of the Lewis and Clark Expedition.* 8 vols. New York: Dodd, Mead, 1904–5.

Chronology

Entries in roman type refer directly to Lewis and Clark and their journey to the Pacific; entries in italics refer to important historical and cultural events of the era.

Aug. 1, 1770	William Clark born in Caroline County, Virginia
Aug. 18, 1774	Meriwether Lewis born in Locust Hill, Virginia
July 4, 1776	*The Declaration of Independence issued*
1781	*British surrender at Yorktown; American Revolution ends*
May 1792	*Robert Gray, American sea captain, discovers Columbia River*
Oct. 1792	*Members of expedition commanded by British mariner George Vancouver sail 150 miles up the Columbia and claim entire region for England*
July 1793	*Fur trader Alexander Mackenzie reaches Pacific Ocean after traveling overland from Lake Athabasca*
1801	*Thomas Jefferson inaugurated president of the United States*
1803	*United States buys the Louisiana Territory from France;* Jefferson charges Lewis and Clark to undertake a "voyage of discovery" to explore the Missouri River in search of a route to the Pacific
Dec. 1803	Lewis and Clark establish winter camp on the Wood River in present-day Illinois
April 1804	Corps of Discovery begins its ascent of the Missouri River
Aug. 1804	First meeting with Indians; Clark holds council with Oto and Missouri
Sept. 1804	Corps has a brush with the Sioux near present-day Pierre, South Dakota
Oct. 1804	Lewis and Clark propose alliance between the warring Hidatsa, Arikara, and Mandan Indians against the Sioux
Nov. 1804	Construction begins on Fort Mandan, the winter headquarters of the Corps of Discovery
April 1805	Trimmed to 33 people, the expedition sets out again up the Missouri

June 1805	Corps makes a month-long portage around the Great Falls of the Missouri
July 1805	Clark falls ill from fatigue after the party reaches the Rocky Mountains
Sept. 1805	Corps traverses the rugged Lolo Trail
Oct. 1805	Navigates rapids on the Columbia
Nov. 1805	Reaches the Pacific Ocean
Dec. 1805	Constructs winter headquarters, Fort Clatsop
July 1806	On return journey, Lewis and Clark divide party; Lewis explores shorter overland routes to the Great Falls and skirmishes with Blackfeet Indians; Clark explores Yellowstone River
Aug. 1806	Corps reunites just south of the Little Knife River and proceeds on to St. Louis

Index

Picture Credits

A. T. Agate, *Chinook Lodge* (#NA3994), Special Collections, University of Washington Libraries: p. 100; American Philosophical Society Library: pp. 104, 105; John James Audubon, courtesy Department Library Services, American Museum of Natural History: pp. 46 *Prairie Wolf* (neg. #2A13268, photo by O. Bauer and J. Beckett), 47 *Prong-horned Antelope* (neg. #322987, photo by R. E. Logan), 69 *Gray Wolf* (neg. #334436, photo by R. E. Logan); John James Audubon, *Prairie Dogs* (#F9703), Denver Public Library, Western History Department: p. 48; *August Chouteau* (artist unknown); Beinecke Library/ Yale University: p. 28; George Caleb Bingham, *Fur Traders Descending the Missouri*, the Bettmann Archive: p. 122; Karl Bodmer, Denver Public Library, Western History Department: pp. 51 *Herds of Buffalo and Elk of the Upper Missouri* (#F28274), 73 *View of the Rocky Mountains* (#F28271), 113 *Bear Hunt on the Missouri* (#F28263); Karl Bodmer, Library of Congress: pp. 55 *Bison Dance of the Mandan Indians* (#LC-USZ62-28806), 61 *The Interior of the Hut of the Mandan Indians* (#LC-USZ62-2086), 88 *Mount Hood from the Columbia* (LC-USZ62-57999), 118 *Encampment of the Pickann Indians Near Fort McKenzie on the Musselshell River* (#LC-USZ62-46118); Karl Bodmer, Rare Book and Manuscript Division, the New York Public Library, Astor, Lenox and Tilden Foundations: pp. 25 *A Blackfoot Indian on Horseback*, 52 *Pehriska Ruhpa in the Costume of the Dog-Band*, 73 *Sih-chida and Machsi-Karehde*, 74 *Mehkckehme-Sukahs*, 80 *View of the Stone Walls*, 126 *Horse Racing of the Sioux Indians*; Karl Bodmer, *Sauk and Fox Indians*, the Bettmann Archive: p. 32; Karl Bodmer, State Historical Society of North Dakota: pp. 40 *Scaffold Burial* (#C-611), 62 *Noapeh* (#C-589), 116 *Arikara Warrior* (#C-585); George Catlin, National Museum of American Art, Washington, DC/Art Resource, NY: pp. 48 *Scalp Dance, Sioux*, 54 *Bird's Eye View of the Mandan River, 1800 Miles Above St. Louis*, 75 *Old Bear*, 76–77 *Bull Dance, Mandan O-Kee-Pa Ceremony*, 121 *River Bluffs, with White Wolves in the Foreground, Upper Missouri*; William Clark, *Flathead Indians* (#ORHI645), Oregon Historical Society: p. 102; Chester Harding, *William Clark*, St. Louis Mercantile Library Association: p. 125; John Wesley Jarvis, *Meriwether Lewis*, Spokane Public Library: p. 12; Paul Kane, courtesy of the Royal Ontario Museum, Toronto, Canada: pp. 95 *The Falls at Coleville on the Columbia River*, 96 *Mount Saint Helens Erupting*, 98 *Cowwachan*; Thomas Lawrence, *Sir Alexander Mackenzie* (#8000), National Gallery of Canada, Ottawa: p. 17; Vikki Leib (map): pp. 18–19; Library, the Academy of Natural Sciences of Philadelphia: pp. 106, 107; Library of Congress: p. 129; Alfred Jacob Miller, Walters Art Gallery, Baltimore: pp. 42 *Pawnee Indians Watching the Caravan*, 65 *Hunting the Bear*, 66–67 *Buffaloes Drinking and Bathing at Night*, 85 *Shoshone Indians Fording a River*, 86 *Presents to the Indians*, 91 *Indian Guide*, 103 *Root Diggers*, 108 *Nez Percé Indian*, 112 *Hunting Elk Among the Black Hills*, 114 *The Blackfeet*; Oregon Historical Society (neg. #ORHI 38090): p. 22; Charles Willson Peale, Independence National Historical Park Collection: cover *Meriwether Lewis*, cover, p. 30 *William Clark*; Alfred Russell, *Louisiana and the Fair* (LC-USZ62-2089), Library of Congress: p. 39; C. M. Russell, Amon Carter Museum, Fort Worth, TX: pp. 58 *The Buffalo Hunt*, 111 *Lewis and Clark on the Lower Columbia*; C. M. Russell, Montana Historical Society, Helena: pp. 56 *York*, 70 *Indians Discovering Lewis and Clark*, 90 *Lewis and Clark Meeting Indians at Ross's Hole*; John Mix Stanley, *Scene on the Columbia River*, Amon Carter Museum, Fort Worth, TX: pp. 78–79; John Mix Stanley *Western Landscape*, © Detroit Institute of Arts, gift of Dexter M. Ferry, Jr.: p. 97; Gilbert Stuart, *Jefferson* (LC-USZ62-54129), Library of Congress: p. 14; Thomas Sully, *Benjamin Rush* (LC-17246), Library of Congress: p. 20; W. Whitteredge, *The Rocky Mountains* (LC-USZ62-42801), Library of Congress: p. 92; J. C. Wild, *View of Front Street*, courtesy Missouri Historical Society, St. Louis: pp. 35, 36; Carl Wimar, *Indians Crossing the Mouth of the Milk River*, Amon Carter Museum, Fort Worth, TX: p. 50

Seamus Cavan has written and edited many books on exploration and American history for young adult readers.

William H. Goetzmann holds the Jack S. Blanton, Sr., Chair in History at the University of Texas at Austin, where he has taught for many years. The author of numerous works on American history and exploration, he won the 1967 Pulitzer and Parkman prizes for his *Exploration and Empire: The Role of the Explorer and Scientist in the Winning of the American West, 1800–1900*. With his son William N. Goetzmann, he coauthored *The West of the Imagination*, which received the Carr P. Collins Award in 1986 from the Texas Institute of Letters. His documentary television series of the same name received a blue ribbon in the history category at the American Film and Video Festival held in New York City in 1987. A recent work, *New Lands, New Men: America and the Second Great Age of Discovery*, was published in 1986 to much critical acclaim.

Michael Collins served as command module pilot on the *Apollo 11* space mission, which landed his colleagues Neil Armstrong and Buzz Aldrin on the moon. A graduate of the United States Military Academy, Collins was named an astronaut in 1963. In 1966 he piloted the *Gemini 10* mission, during which he became the third American to walk in space. The author of several books on space exploration, Collins was director of the Smithsonian Institution's National Air and Space Museum from 1971 to 1978 and is a recipient of the Presidential Medal of Freedom.